WEEKEND CANOEING IN MICH
THE RIVERS, THE TOWNS, THE TAVERNS

Doc Fletcher

Arbutus Press
Traverse City, Michigan

Weekend Canoeing in Michigan: The Rivers, The Towns, The Taverns
© Doc Fletcher, 2008, 2017

ISBN 13 - 978-1-933926-09-4

Tenth Anniversary Edition

Arbutus Press
Traverse City, Michigan
editor@arbutuspress.com
www.Arbutuspress.com

Second Edition/ Second Printing

Printed and bound in the United States of America

Data source for maps: 2006 ESRI Data and Maps and Michigan Center for Geographic Information.
Map GIS specialist Paul Reiss, Land Information Access Association.

Maps © Arbutus Press, 2008
Illustrations © Keith Jones, 2008
Photos © Doc Fletcher, 2008

DEDICATION

To Maggie,
whose love, warmth, hugs, smiles and patience sustain me.

4

"EVERYONE MUST BELIEVE IN SOMETHING.
I BELIEVE I'LL GO CANOEING"

Henry David Thoreau

CONTENTS

UPPER PENINSULA RIVERS

LOWER PENINSULA RIVERS

PREFACE

The wonderful folks of the great state of Michigan are blessed with an abundance of fabulous rivers—among the state's other natural treasures. This book looks at twenty Michigan rivers and focuses on small segments of rivers, referred to as the "suggested trips".

THE CRITERIA TO FEATURE A SUGGESTED TRIP IN A PARTICULAR RIVER WAS THE FOLLOWING:

• must be serviced by a canoe livery, as the book is for the weekend warriors many of whom do not own their own canoe,
• should have at least some stretches of fast water or white water
• if possible, be a on relatively unknown river or be an underused stretch – a "hidden gem"
• with very few exceptions, a river that is not too crowded
• be a trip that I'd look forward to a return trip

Over 30 years of canoeing with friends and family, the question asked countless times: "How much further do we have to go?" This book provides landmarks along each river to answer that question such as a log leaning in from the left shore that is 1 hour into a 3 hour trip, or a large creek merging into the river that is 45 minutes into a 2 hour trip.

EACH CHAPTER PROVIDES DETAILS TO HELP YOU PLAN YOUR TRIP INCLUDING:

• miles to the river from various Michigan towns–and from Milwaukee, home of Pabst Blue Ribbon Beer.
• a canoe livery servicing each river, with phone number, address, and website.
• degree of difficulty (beginner/moderate/veteran) suggested for paddling each river.
• the background trip overview.
• trip outline of the river giving you suggested trips and outlining the time to complete the trip. Also we provide landmarks to determine the progression such as speed, depth, width of the river, obstacles you'll encounter, and camping locations.
• "the tavern" suggests where to grab a bite and a beer after the trip.
• "the town" starts off with the local Detroit Tigers radio affiliate (Go Get 'Em Tigers!), and continues with interesting historical tidbits.

CHAPTERS INCLUDE OUR SOUNDTRACK FOR EACH RIVER

The music may be inspired by some characteristic of that river and the river quotes from the suggested river trip. Quote Warning: some quotes may have been chosen due to lack of material to work with.

INTRODUCTION

I love Michigan - born, raised, and lived my whole life here – the saying "smitten by the mitten" fits me to a T.

I love canoeing Michigan's rivers - a love affair that began with my first canoe trip down the Pere Marquette River in 1978.

The purpose of this book is not to provide the reader with a detailed canoeing analysis of virtually every Michigan river in both peninsulas — that was already done in a wonderful book,"Canoeing Michigan Rivers", by Jerry Dennis and Craig Date. No, this book is meant for the casual canoeist who is looking for a fun 2-4 hour canoe trip that can be extended to a full day or two through extended breaks to toss the Frisbee, grab a sandwich, and sip a cold one.

ACKNOWLEDGEMENTS

I would like to express my deepest gratitude to the folks at the Pabst Blue Ribbon Brewing Co. The blue ribbon was awarded to PBR – despite fierce competition – at the 1893 World's Fair.

Thanks are also extended to those fine battery-makin' folks at Duracell, who allowed me to make a wonderful living for 30 years, introduced me to many, many life-long friends, and who financially allowed me the time to research and write this book.

And thanks to my Mom and Dad, for lots of love and direction -and for holding the bike upright until I could ride it myself.

THE FOX RIVER
SENEY, MICHIGAN

Level Two
Tricky

Level 2, moderate ability to
Level 3, veteran ability

Level THREE
Veteran

Fox River soundtrack:
16 Tons – TE Ford
White Sport Coat – Marty Robbins, Men – Martin Mull
Roger Miller medley: King Of The
Road/ Dang Me/ Chug-A-Lug
Two Rivers – Brian Flechsig and Charlie Weaver

Canoe livery:
Northland Outfitters, owners Leon and Donna Genre
8174 Hwy M-77
Germfask, Michigan 49836.
Phone (906) 586-9801, www.northoutfitters.com.

THE BACKGROUND

The Fox is serviced by Northland Outfitters in Germfask. From the Mackinac Bridge, take US2 65 miles west to the US2 and M77 junction. Follow M77 north for 10 miles. The Fox is fast-flowing, cold, tight shore-to-shore, and presents many of nature's obstacles. The Fox River has uncommon beauty.

In his youth, Ernest Hemingway camped along the Fox River and found its fishing wonderful, prompting him to write the short story *Big Two Hearted River,* in 1924. Hemingway borrowed the more romantic sounding name of another Upper Peninsula river for the title of his story, in which he recounts his Fox River adventures.

The vast majority of this book's "suggested trips" takes you on a 1 day adventure (although two exceptions are found in the first 2 chapters: on the Fox and the Manistique Rivers). The 1-day trips are detailed on both rivers and also outlined are the 4-day trips that I've taken, on either the Fox or the Manistique, annually (except in 1984) since 1978.

Joining me on the Fox for the book research: Dr. Bob Kocembo, Johnny Steck, Neal Linkon, Kenny Umphrey, Gomie (Shoeless Pat) Carroll, Vid Marvin, Jason Brown, Marc Weaks, Gary Gillam, Chris Weaks, Ron Swiecki, Matthew Rose, and Jeff Cripe.

THE RIVER: THE FOX

Suggested 4 day trip puts in a 3 hour float north of Seney, taking the river until it's junction with the Manistique, ending 2 hours downstream from the junction, at the Northland Outfitters canoe livery. Total actual float time over the 4 days is 15 hours.

Day 1 is the 3 hour/7 miles from the Fox River Campground ending at the Seney Township Campsite, the only civilized campsite (ie, other people and outhouses) on this Fox River trip. This day features a few tricky turns including *Russell's Corner* where, in his glory days, big Russell flipped his boat back-to-back years (430 pounds hitting the water rocks boats quite a distance away), but for the most part this section of the Fox is a level 2 stretch of moderate difficulty. In some early day 1 locations, the river is so tight from shore to shore that a canoe turned sideways can stop all other traffic.

The day 1 current is swift, the average shore-to-shore width of the river is 15' to 20', the bottom is sandy, and locations to pull over your canoe for a break are somewhat limited. Water levels range from knee deep to over your head, averaging 4' deep.

The Seney Township campsite will be on your right. This site has plenty of camping, two outhouses, fire pits, and pump water. A large island fronts the Township site, which we have used for our camping most years (as the main site can be crowded). Andy's Seney Bar (see "The Tavern") is less than a two-mile walk from the site. Downstream from here you're in the wilderness (no official campsites, bathrooms, or other forms of civilization) with no chance to exit the river until you reach Northland Outfitters livery in Germfask.

Day 2 key landmarks….

~~   20 minutes in, float beneath the M-28 bridge.
~~   45 minutes in, the start of the *Spreads* (detailed below)
~~   1 hour 15 minutes in, the end of the *Spreads*, logjams soon begin
~~   5 hours in, clearing with defaced birch on right bank
~~   6 hours in, High Ground campsite on the left (detailed below)

Day 2 is 6 hours of rough canoeing known affectionately as "hell day", with a level 3 degree of difficulty – veteran ability required. Beginning about 90 minutes in, through Day 2's end, the canoeing takes you through a series of logjams that often stretch from shore-to-shore. The number of logjams varies (12 is a common number), in part, on the severity of the previous winter's storms. Many logjams feature a fallen tree blocking the river shore-to-shore, its trunk sticking 1-2 feet above the water surface, with many branches fanning out from the trunk. The canoeist is forced to pull up their boat alongside the tree trunk, get out of the canoe while climbing on to the trunk, find the tree's path of least resistance, and pull the canoe through that path to the river waiting on the other side. It is strongly suggested that you make this maneuver with the help of other canoeists in order to (1) assist in pushing your canoe over the tree trunks, especially if it's weighed down with 4 days of supplies, and (2) to grab the canoe after it splashes down on the tree trunk's other side so that the 4 days of supplies may be enjoyed by you and not wildlife downstream. Day 2 water depth ranges primarily from neck to knee deep.

Upon reaching the campsite at the end of these 6 hours, the normal person (as well as my friends) will be absolutely exhausted, aching to the bone, after working their way down this stretch of the river. The end is a campsite known as *"the High Ground"*, a 4' high elevated and cleared dirt-floor piece of land. The High Ground is on the left shore at the end of a long straight-away, and is populated with tall, leafless trees and mosquitoes. You will sleep well.

So why go through "hell day?" First, the shared struggle is akin to a barn raising, and is a great bonding experience – although it can be hard to see this benefit at logjam number 10. Beyond the bonding is the unique beauty of day 2, best captured by the section of the Fox known as *"the Spreads"*. At the mouth of the Spreads, the river splits in two, and that split again splits in two, and this repeats itself again and again over the next 30 minutes of canoeing. You can follow any of the splits in the river, and magically meet up with your fellow floaters as the Spreads come to an end. While traversing the Spreads, you can reach out from your canoe with either your left hand or your right hand and touch the bushes on each shore. As the width of the Fox is squeezed, the river picks up speed and you have the feeling of being on an amusement park ride as you travel the rushing S-curves. Fortunately, there are no logjams through this stretch of great beauty and great fun. We have found that, although you cannot see friends who travel different splits during their trip through the Spreads, having one canoe with their radio tuned loudly to the Detroit Tigers baseball game keeps us all in contact with each other as sound travels well through the Spreads.

Day 3 is a two-hour trip from the High Ground to the *Peninsula*. A few of the logjams experienced on day 2 remain, but for the most part it's a leisurely journey. Water depth varies from ankle deep to over your head deep. The Peninsula camping area may be entered from either side of the Peninsula, with both entry points on your right, the 2nd entry point the easier of the two landings. This camp area is as large - we've set up 6 or more tents with plenty of space between - as it is scenic. Many years we've incorporated this 2- hour trip with the day 2 float (if we have enough daylight left), and use day 3 to stay in camp all day for relaxing, swimming, and general kicking back.

Day 4 key landmarks…

~~   1 hour 30 minutes in, the Fox East Branch merges slowly from your left.
~~   2 hours in, float below the new steel bridge.
~~   100 yards beyond the bridge, the Manistique River rolls in from the left as it merges with the Fox River - the trip's end, and the livery, is now 1 hour and 40 minutes away.

~~   3 hours in (45 minutes from today's end) just beyond a right bend in the river sits a 120' long sandy beach on the right shore, known as Moth's Landing.

~~   3 hours, 25 minutes in (20 minutes from the end) is a very large home on your left where the river bends to the right.

~~   3 hours 40 minutes in (5 minutes from the end) is an island – you may float the quiet current to the right or take the light rapids on the left. The livery take out will be on your right.

Day 2 through 4 runs 11.5 hours/16 miles

At the Manistique and Fox merger, you can stand with one leg in each river, and clearly note how much colder the Fox is versus the Manistique. About 100 yards before this merger is the new steel bridge, which in the Spring of 1992 replaced the (and sung with great gusto) *Old…Log…Bridge*. The lack of capital letters when writing the "new steel bridge" reflects the disdain our veteran paddlers have for the loss of our beautiful Old Log Bridge, not considered progress in our book. Ok, I'm done. The Old Log Bridge did, and now the new steel bridge does, serve as a wonderful location to take a fine, long break before the trip's end, and very effectively lighten the weight of coolers while engaging in the social activities of sharing food and drink, storytelling, and laughter. Debarking from the new steel bridge and back in your canoe, there remains the final 100 yards of the Fox and, after the merger with the Manistique, the final 1 hour 40 minute float to the livery. The river gets wide and slow, average depth waist to armpit, as you float towards the canoe livery. 45 minutes from the end, around a bend to your right, you'll come upon an unmarked historical site, a 120' long, sandy beach - *Moth's Landing*. If taking a swim break here DO NOT dive in head first. Large tree roots sticking out of the river's bottom here will get you a head wound.

Late afternoon from Moth's Landing to the canoe livery is heaven on earth. The sun-drenched colors are their most vivid. You have that light sun burnt warmth from a satisfying journey, the cigar's half smoked, and it seems that the river has no end. The scene will make non-believers offer up a prayer of thanks.

THE TOWN: SENEY

Detroit Tigers local radio affiliate: WNBY 1450AM (Newberry).

During it's logging heyday of the 1880s and 1890s, no town in the entire USA was more colorful than little Seney, Michigan. At that time, home to about 3,000 folks, 25 or so liquor establishments, and 5 brothels, Seney was the place to go for hard work, hard play, and mayhem. Few residents were wilder than P.K. Small, who greeted folks taking the train through town by turning them upside down and shaking from their pockets a "loose offering" before sending them on their way. The 1891 blood feud between the Harcourts and the Dunns lives on a century later, as we found out one afternoon while relaxing in Andy's Bar – our dear, late buddy Goobs was having a pleasant chat with a local old-timer, until Goobs mentioned that he knew a fella by the name of Harcourt that used to have relatives in the area. Without saying another word, the older gent just turned his back on Goober, and the pleasant bar talk was at an end.

The feud came to a head as the result of the 1891 shooting of Steve Harcourt by Dan Dunn, and the revenge killing of Dan Dunn by Jim Harcourt. After Jim's release from prison in 1894, the people of Seney made their statement on the feud, electing Jim Harcourt to supervisor for nine terms. When the lumbermen took the last stand of white pine at the close of the 19th century, the town began the metamorphosis into what you see today: 250 folks in a quiet village only interrupted by the Fox River, talk and laughter in Andy's Bar, big rigs blowing by on M28, and populated in part by Mennonites that have moved into Seney and established an outreach ministry.

Sources: "Incredible Seney" by Lewis C. Reimann, bar talk, Johnny Harcourt

THE TAVERN: ANDY'S SENEY BAR

Less than a 2-mile walk from the Seney Township Campsite along the Fox River, Andy's sits on M28 just east of the Fox. Although the prices have changed since we immortalized Andy's in a 1985 song, the philosophy remains the same: "At $1.50 a pitcher your money goes far, but we still dropped fifty at Andy's – Andy's Seney Bar". We've never sent Andy's food back, the locals have treated us warmly and with concern ("Say buddy, do you think your friend will fall off the bar stool?"), the legendary Banjo Bob lived nearby in his car and would regale us with song for shots, and Andy himself bought us many a rounds while sharing a laugh with us. Andy's is a small bar with a big heart – and here's an example: the Colonel and Marty stopped by Andy's on the way home to the Detroit area from a snowmobiling trip in the U.P. a few years back. They planned to split a shot and a beer, as they didn't have the money left for one each. Andy didn't

15

THE MANISTIQUE RIVER
GERMFASK, MICHIGAN

Level One
Beginner Ability Required

Level 1, easy, to Level 2, moderate ability

Level Two
Tricky

Manistique River soundtrack:
Big Rock Candy Mountain - Harry McClintock
Lunatic Fringe - Red Rider
A Very Good Beer - Homer Simpson
Delia - Johnny Cash
I like Beer - Tom T. Hall

Canoe livery: Northland Outfitters
owners Leon and Donna Genre
8174 Hwy M-77 ~ Germfask, Michigan 49836
Phone 906~586~9801
www.northoutfitters.com

THE BACKGROUND

The Manistique is serviced by Northland Outfitters in Germfask. Once over the Mackinac Bridge, go 65 miles west on US2 until the US2-M77 junction. Go north on M77 10 miles. The Manistique is slower, warmer, wider, and a more relaxing float than the Fox, with which it converges two floating hours to the east of Germfask. During the last 2 days of this suggested 4 day trip, another canoe is rarely seen, evoking the spirit of the late John Voelker, author and State Supreme Court Judge from Marquette, Michigan, who wrote in his book *Trout Madness,* "...because only in the woods can I find solitude without loneliness... because bourbon out of an old tin cup always taste better out there."

Joining me on the Manistique for the book research: Dr. Bob Kocembo, Johnny Steck, Neal Linkon, Kenny Umphrey, Gomie (Shoeless Pat) Carroll, Vid Marvin, Jason Brown, Marc Weaks, Gary Gillam, Chris Weaks, Ron Swiecki, Matthew Rose, and Jeff Cripe.

THE RIVER: THE MANISTIQUE

The suggested 4 day trip puts in at Ten Curves Road, a 2.5 hour float just northeast of Germfask and the Northland Outfitters canoe livery, ending another 10 hours downstream past the livery at the Cookson Bridge take-out point. Total actual float time over the 4 days is 12 and one-half hours. Each day the river is (except for a dam 30 minutes into day 1 of the trip) portage free, 60' to 90' shore-to-shore, featuring a primarily sandy bottom that lends itself to canoeing breaks for Frisbee tossing. Along the river, we've seen everything from eagles (frequently) to bear cubs and, even once, a cow !

Day 1 is a 2.5 hour, 6 mile, trip ending at the canoe livery, a fully-furnished campsite, i.e., real sit- down toilets, designated camp areas, convenience store, and a short ½ mile walk to the Jolly Bar (see "Taverns" section). The first hour of today's trip is a... very... slow, slow... float. In fact, when you first put in at Ten Curves, it's a reasonable question to ask do we go left or right? The answer is right.

30 minutes into the trip you'll come to a small dam that will require a portage. At the left bank is a wonderful tribute from the Ten Curves Club to a fallen comrade – check it out. After the dam, the river current picks up slightly and you're now 20 minutes from the junction with the Fox River–where the Fox River ends as it merges with the Manistique.

Now, before you follow the left-hand turn downstream at this merger, I suggest that you make a right-hand detour and paddle 100 yards against the Fox current, canoe under the new steel bridge, pulling over on the right bank just beyond it. Grab a beer from your cooler, a cigar from your dry box, get out of your canoe, climb up the bridge, grab a seat to relax and watch two beautiful rivers merge and flow in a gorgeous setting. Before resuming canoeing, pay homage with song to the new steel bridge predecessor the *Old ...Log... Bridge......*

Now, doesn't that feel good?

From the Manistique-Fox merger to the canoe livery campsite is 1 hour and 40 minutes, and constitutes the only stretch that is traveled on both the Fox and the Manistique trips with the livery. The Manistique picks up speed, but only a little, after its merger with the Fox River. The river depth the balance of day 1 averages waist deep. 20 minutes from the livery lies a large home on your left. 5 minutes from the end is an island, calm water to the right and a fun light rapids run on the left. The livery take out will be 5 minutes downstream on the right.

Day 2 is a 4 hour, 10 mile, trip from Northland Outfitters to the Mead Creek Campsite. When our Florida friends asked for clarification of the campground name, it was suggested that they refer back to a July 1863 day at Gettysburg, when their ancestors ran up a hill and the campground's namesake kicked their butts (slight difference in spelling, but they seemed to understand). On a river, that kind of comment is an oar of northern aggression.

During the first 45 minutes of today's trip, you'll canoe under two bridges at Ten Curves Road and M77. In low water, there are three sets of light rapids between the livery and the M77 Bridge. Passing under M77 marks your entry into the Seney National Wildlife Refuge. I'd point out what a beautiful stretch the Refuge is, but the whole river is a beautiful stretch (canoeing wisdom: when you have a cooler full of ice-cold Pabsts, the most beautiful one is the one you're holding).

Today's current speed is moderate, no major obstacles, no portages, with depths of 2' to 6' for the most part. Once inside the Wildlife Refuge, three waterways, each marked with a sign, will enter the river from your right: Gray's Creek, Pine Creek, and Drigg's River. Gray's Creek is today's 1/3rd mark, Pine Creek is the half-way mark, and Drigg's River is 15 minutes from Mead Creek, which will be on your left. The Mead Creek Campsite landmark is a concrete ramp. The takeout is next to the ramp. ***Warning***: while Mead is a comfortable camp setting (complete with regularly cleaned outhouses), there is a fair amount of poison ivy present, *leaves of 3, let it be*. Scout out your tent setup and walking areas while there is daylight to minimize the need for an ocean of calamine lotion later.

Days 3 and 4 combined took our group 6 hours to canoe the 15 miles from the Mead Creek Campground to the Cookson Bridge takeout. Mead Creek is both the end of the Seney Wildlife Refuge and the start of the Manistique River State Forest. This stretch features the river at its widest and, except for our singing, the quietest. Shoving off from Mead, the Manistique River is the definition of peaceful: clouds over the tree line looks like a Colorado Mountain range… rarely is another canoe seen on this stretch… just the wind blowing through the trees and the sun glistening off of the river. The other lasting memory is the incredible height of the ancient and beautiful trees along the shoreline.

Several waterways merge with the Manistique, all unmarked. The times from the Mead Creek Campsite: merging from the right is Marsh Creek -1 hr 15 min, from the left is Mezik Creek – 1 hr 40 min, from the right merges Dougal Creek – 3 hr 15 min from Mead. 5 minutes beyond Dougal Creek sits a house with a cable car that goes across the river.

Long sandy beaches seen in some numbers before Mead are in much greater numbers downstream from Mead. These offer excellent camping opportunities. We chose to camp at a sandy beach 10 minutes past Dougal Creek. ***Please note:*** As there are no established campsites between Mead and Cookson, finding a campsite for the night on Day 3 depends a great deal on the water level. If the river is running low, there will be plenty of sandy beaches that will do just fine, but if the water is running high, don't be too picky about where you stay. If it's getting late in the afternoon, grab the next acceptable location.

The lack of work required to push downstream, combined with the relatively long time on the river, leads to a great deal of story-telling among the boats as we float together on days 3 and 4. In 1716, Antoine de la Mothe Cadillac wrote the following regarding the men of the Upper Peninsula which offers a good summation of tales told: "A certain proof of the excellence of the climate is to see the old men there, whose grandsons are growing grey; it would seem as if death had no power to carry off these spectors. They have good hearing and good sight, but their memory often plays them tricks. They tell tales and recount events which they maintain happened at the time, which is not credible, but they have this advantage that there is no one who can contradict them or call them liars except by inference."

4 hr 15 min downstream from Mead, a beautiful little creek flows into the river from the left, just before the corrugated shack on the left shore. 5 hr 30 min from Mead, on a bend, merges a 3' wide creek from the right, dropping down over two rock ledges before entering the Manistique. 15 minutes before the Cookson Bridge take out, immediately beyond a gorgeous 150' long sandy beach, the 20' wide Duck Creek flows into the river from the right. The steep Cookson Bridge take out is just past the bridge on the left.

THE TOWNS: CURTIS & GERMFASK

Detroit Tigers local radio affiliate: WNBY 1450AM (Newberry).

Curtis: 4,000 acres of water in the Little Manistique Lake (south of Curtis)… 7,000 acres of water in Big Manistique Lake (north of Curtis). State road H42 runs east and west through Curtis, providing both the dividing line between the Big and Little (aka South) Manistique Lakes, as well as the main road on which sits the vast majority of Curtis' lodging, bars, restaurants, and shops. A stroll down H42 gives you the sensation of a trip back in time, taking your mind to an enjoyable day in the 1940s or 50s. The Lakes provide excellent boating, canoeing, and fishing – including pike, walleye, perch, and whitefish – as well as snowmobiling in a beautiful scenic setting. To prep you for a full day of fun, we've found that an excellent breakfast can be had at Stamper's Restaurant, a short walk east of Mc's Tally Ho.

Sources: Curtis Chamber of Commerce, bar talk

Germfask: The name Germfask was derived from the first initial in the last name of the eight families that founded the town in 1881. During FDR years, a piece of property just south of town was used as a Civilian Conservation Corps camp. In 1944 and 1945, this same piece of land became one of four Michigan camps for World War II conscientious objectors. Today, the town is home to several churches, no gas stations, and only a handful of businesses beyond the Northland Outfitters canoe livery and the Jolly Motel and Bar.
The good folks of Germfask seem to think that this quiet life goes along quite nicely with the peaceful flow of the Manistique River, disturbed only by those tourists who drive up M77 to share in the natural beauty Germfask is blessed with.

Sources: David Hacker 1990 Detroit Free Press article, bar talk

THE TAVERNS: MC'S TALLY HO - CURTIS, JOLLY BAR - GERMFASK

The road to the 4Day runs through a Friday night in the U.P. town of Curtis and sits at a table near the end of the bar at Betsy's Mc's Tally Ho. Betsy McCormick was proprietor from 1974 to 2001 of what we've found to be the most welcoming bar in the U.P., Mc's Tally Ho. Beginning in 1994, the eve of our Manistique or Fox trips would be spent in the warmth of Betsy's saloon, and she always made our group of "down below" visitors feel as welcome as if we were at our own hometown bar. Betsy would always inquire as to when she could expect us on our annual trip, to ensure sufficient quantities of food, Pabst Blue Ribbons, Cuervo, and Beam were stocked. Betsy was larger than life, seemed to make a friend everywhere she ventured, and passed away the evening of 9/23/01 in a most fitting way: during a night on the town among those she loved, she got up to dance and died instantly of a heart attack. A short time later, Kim Bushy became the new owner. The cosmetic changes since 2001 reflect the different styles of the two ladies, but Kim has successfully maintained the Mc's Tally Ho's welcoming atmosphere.

Jolly Bar – Germfask One-half mile to the south of Northland Outfitters in Germfask sits the Jolly Bar. Through a variety of owners over our 40 years of paddling in the area, we've found travelers are welcomed here, the staff makes sure patron beers are kept full, and the food served is consistently good (including on Pizza Night each Tuesday). Right next to the bar is the Jolly Rose Motel. Owner Rose and her dog, Pete Rose, are genuinely happy to see us each year, and she keeps the rustic, log cabin-style, rooms lookin' good. For our money, you won't see finer accommodations in your U.P. travels. Call Rose at (906) 586-6385, www.jollyrosemotel.com.

.

THE MICHIGAMME RIVER
CRYSTAL FALLS, MICHIGAN

Level Two
Tricky

level 2,
Moderate ability required

Michigamme River soundtrack:
Roll Out the Barrel – Frankie Yankovic,
Many Rivers to Cross – Jimmy Cliff,
If You Wanna Get to Heaven – Ozark Mountain
Daredevils , Hillbilly Hula Gal – Junior Brown,
Beer Run – Todd Snider

Canoe livery: Michi-Aho Resort
owners Pat and Judy Hingos
2181 Highway M-69 ~ (at the Michigamme River
Bridge, 6 miles east of Crystal Falls,)
Crystal Falls, Michigan 49920
Phone 906~875-3514
www.michi-aho.com

THE BACKGROUND

Short, sweet, and unexpected best sums up our trip down the Michigamme River…

<u>Short</u> because the projected 3 hour trip surprisingly ended at 1 hour and 20 minutes to cover its 4.5 miles.

<u>Sweet</u> because of the many light rapids, the enjoyable challenge presented by the rocks located throughout the river, the fascinating history of the area, and that Pat Hingos and his Michi-Aho Resort turned out to be excellent hosts.

<u>Unexpected</u> because the Michigamme was not on the original 20-river itinerary. Another Upper Peninsula river, the Ford, was the scheduled river at this point in our adventure. However, dry conditions made the Ford water level too low to float a canoe. Although I look forward to a future Ford River trip, the dry conditions were our good fortune as the Michigamme was a real treat – and will be for you, too.

THE RIVER: THE MICHIGAMME

The suggested trip begins at Hemlock Dam, ending at the M-69 Bridge (taking out at the Michi-Aho Resort). There are no public toilets, no portages, no good pullover points for breaks, plenty of light rapids, and MANY rocks along this stretch of the Michigamme.

As soon as we put in, there is a large island to canoe around so pass on the right, as the left is too shallow. The first set of light rapids is immediately past the island.

15 minutes in, a dead creek very slowly merges from the right. 2 minutes later, a creek rolls in from the left.

30 minutes in, on the right, sits an alcove that is 100' deep and 70' across. Continuing downstream, just beyond the alcove, is an island. Fronting the island is a piece of driftwood 30' long, nice enough that it may not be there next trip through. Pass the island on the left – the river is very shallow on the right, shallow enough that a walk through may be required.

This is a river about rocks. They predominate throughout. The rocks are first noticed at the base of the above mentioned island. The rocks are along both shorelines, at the bottom of the river, and sticking out above the water line. The rocks range in size from small enough to fit in the palm of your hand to 4' wide.

Beyond the island is an 80' to 100' long rapids run along a very rocky river bottom. You will bump and bounce your way through this a very enjoyable section of the Michigamme trip. The river seems to drop a few inches as you enter these rapids. Over the next 200', there are rocks on the left and rapids on the right (for fun, go right!). After a 200' stretch of calm water, there's a light rapids run of 70'. Around the next bend, class 1 rock-infested rapids take you to the Old 69 Bridge (near the 1893 mine disaster).

Whitewater just before the bridge created waves that crested above the top of our canoes.

Shiver me timbers and knock me down mate! 2 bends past the bridge, is a 250' run of light rapids. Around the next bend you enter a rock garden featuring a big rock that knocked me off of my seat and the paddle out of my hands (very cool!). The rocks come at you with speed and frequency, adding to the thrill of the ride.

Just beyond the rock garden, on the river's right, lies a little gravel island with flowers. Pass the island on the left as the right appears un-navigable.

50 and 55 minutes in, creeks enter the Michigamme on a severe diagonal from the right. Between these 2 creeks is a very large, wide island – passable on both the left and right.

1 hour in: from this point on, the river deepens and homes begin to appear with regularity.

1 hour 20 minutes in, the trip concludes at the M-69 Bridge. Just before the bridge, exit the river on the right. A small channel leads to the Michi-Aho boat launch and take-out.

THE TOWN: CRYSTAL FALLS

Detroit Tigers local radio affiliate: WDMJ 1320AM (Marquette).

The town of Crystal Falls is located 10 miles directly north of the Michigan-Wisconsin border, and 35 minutes northwest of Iron Mountain. Its name is derived from the falls of the nearby Paint River. Crystal Falls serves as the county seat of Iron County, a county built from "the iron and the pine."

The land that makes up Iron County was a part of Marquette and Menominee counties until 1885, at which time Iron County was created from a portion of the land of both. Iron ore deposits, which gave the new county its name, were the first on the Menominee Iron Range to be discovered. The logging of the pines began in 1875 and, up until 1882, dominated the economy and created work for all who wanted a job. By 1882, the railroad came through this area, and ore shipping could commence – and logging, while still vital to the economy, was now second in importance to iron ore mining.

Iron River was the first county seat of Iron County. By 1889, the government was shifted to Crystal Falls. Work soon commenced on the county courthouse in what is now the historic district of Crystal Falls, constructed of regional materials including reddish stone columns quarried from the Paint River. Completed in 1891 and providing a fabulous view of the city's main street, the valley to the east, and the entire surrounding area, the courthouse is the most architecturally significant building in the county. Built when iron was king, and with its domed courtroom, this beautiful building remains the county courthouse over a century later.

Sources: Michigan History Division, Department of State, www.upheritage.org.

THE TAVERN:
THE INFIELD BAR

Just outside and to the left of the Infield Bar's front door, we're greeted with these words, "On this site in 1897, nothing happened". Once inside, we see that behind the bar a Pabst Blue Ribbon (available in cans only) light wears a blue hula skirt. Oh yeah, a neon sign says "pizzeria" above the front door. We're sold.

The Infield has a definite 1950's feel to it. The glass block looking outdoors is very cool. The only menu item is thin crust pizza – that'll do just fine for folks just off of the river. It's clear that everyone standing up at the bar (where there are few open spaces) knows each other real well - great friends having a great party. The few folks sitting at tables (including us) are just as clearly not part of the party, but are greatly entertained by just watching it unfold.

When the Infield juke box plays a polka song, which happens frequently, the regulars back away from the bar to dance. They also set up an unspoken rotation to play the single instrument on hand, known by 2 different names: a polka-cello OR a stump-fiddle, which is basically a cane with a tambourine and a cowbell on it. The musical ability of these players seems to improve as our stay in the bar lengthens. The pool table and dart board were just for décor during our visit – 'cause it was dancing time!

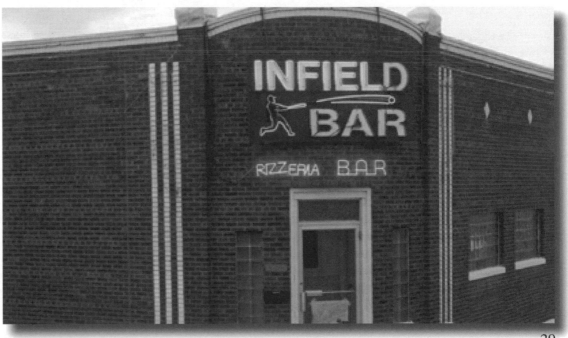

ONTONAGON RIVER
WATERSMEET, MICHIGAN

Level THREE Veteran

level 3 veteran ability suggested

Ontonagon River soundtrack:
Tumbling Dice – Stones,
Nine Below Zero– Sonny Boy Williamson,
Brahma Fear– Jimmy Buffett,
Give Me Back My Wig– Hound Dog Taylor,
Honky Tonk Man– Sleepy Labeef

Canoe livery:
Sylvania Outfitters,
owner Bob Zelinski,
E23423 US Hwy 2, Watersmeet, Michigan 49969.
Phone (906) 358-4766.
www.sylvaniaoutfitters.com

THE BACKGROUND

One of the greatest canoe trips I've ever been on was the 1984 4Day adventure down the Middle Branch of the Ontonagon. As years went on, that trip's swarms of mosquitoes, plagues of black flies, and onslaught of giant deer flies receded in our memories (a bit), and the thrill of the Ontonagon's rapids came to the forefront ("What a terrible thing to have lost one's mind. Or not to have a mind at all. How true that is. " - Dan Quayle). The Middle Branch of the Ontonagon is a river that draws you back to canoe again regardless of the 560 mile drive from home.

There are two wonderful canoe trips that are suggested on the Ontonagon which - with a break at Burned Dam Falls - can be done in back-to-back days…

Day 1 ran west of Watersmeet (putting in right across Hwy 2 from Sylvania Outfitters) to the Burned Dam Falls campsite. This stretch of the river is surrounded by marshland, fed by streams and creeks numbering in the dozens. We enjoyed 5 sets of rapids that require, for the most part, veteran canoeing abilities. The canoeing time was 4 hours 45 minutes to cover 9 miles.

Day 2 ran from the Burned Dam Falls campsite to Interior Bridge. Here the river offers a fantastic downhill run as the Middle Branch drops 40' over a 6 mile stretch, during which we flew through 7 sets of rapids that had us shouting throughout! (now THIS is fun!!!). The total day 2 canoeing time ran exactly 2 hours.

We suggest wearing life jackets during both days. When the canoe livery owner, very aware that we're veterans, thinks we should wear life jackets, well… he knows the river a lot better than we do. Our foursome had over 75 years of canoeing experience, and we think Bob made the right call.

31

THE RIVER: MIDDLE BRANCH OF THE ONTONAGON

The suggested trip is a 2 day adventure: day 1 runs from 1 mile west of Watersmeet to the Burned Dam Falls, and day 2 from Burned Dam to the Interior Bridge, with a combined two day total canoeing time of 6 hours and 45 minutes. The only toilets or designated camp sites over the 2 days is at the Burned Dam Falls campgrounds.

Day 1 we put in just north of Highway 2, and 1 mile west of Highway 45, across Hwy 2 from Sylvania Outfitters. Here the river is 20' wide and half-a-foot deep. 1' tall reeds populate the river bottom, and there is some bottom skimming of rocks.

7 minutes in, a fallen tree allows you only a 3' canoeing opening along the right bank.
8 minutes in, a creek merges from the right – the first of many today, about 8' wide at its junction with the Ontonagon, with a swampy, bayou look to it. After the creek merges, the river widens to 30' across, and we travel through the first rock garden of the day.

The rock garden rocks protrude above the river's surface anywhere from barely visible to a foot or more above the water line. They're placed in a haphazard manner along both straight-aways and bends – as if God had the rocks in a large dice cup, gave 'em a good shake and let 'em fly. The rock gardens add an enjoyably challenging element to the trip, as you cut back left, right, left, etc., navigating your canoe through the equivalent of an enormous pinball machine layout.

15 minutes in, the river width tightens to 20' wide and will, for the most part, vary all day long within the 20' to 40' wide range. You next come upon a man-made rock ledge - with an interesting formation on the river's right - that we had to (ironically) rock our canoes off of. This is followed by another rock ledge 25 minutes in.

30 minutes in, a creek merges from the right that creates a sand bar on the river's edge.

40 minutes in, trees lean in from each shore providing a beautiful canopy effect. This is reminiscent of the dark beauty of Spanish moss trees bending over a street in Savannah.

45 minutes in, we reach the first of two bridges that are 100' feet apart. On the approach to the 1st bridge is a rock ledge that creates a 4" drop in the water – it's suggested that you canoe right through the river's middle (just follow the "v" in the current). You should navigate the rocks at the 2nd bridge - the Highway 45 bridge – by canoeing to their left.

Just past the Hwy 45 bridge, you'll reach a grassy peninsula (with rental cabins on the high ground) – stay to the left. The water merging from the right adds enough additional volume to temporarily deepen the river to 12", minimizing (again, temporarily) bottom skimming.

Big rocks on the river bottom alternate with a sand-gravel mix.

Canoeing Wisdom sidebar: *When it appeared that our trip would end well before the scheduled pick up time, I suggested that we could spend the wait playing cards and drinking beer. Kenny showed the wisdom from years on the river and replied, "Speed up!"*

Trout rearing station from the 1930s 1 hour 40 minutes in, we pass two sets of concrete pillars, each 3' wide, supporting… nothing. As you pass between the pillars – your only option – the Ontonagon drops 3" or 4", creating a short-lived rapids. Bob Zelinski informed us that this is the remains of a trout rearing station built during the 1930s. Back then, the space between the pillars was covered with screens, making for <u>very</u> effective fishing in the days when money for a meal was hard to come by.

1 hour 50 minutes in – 10 minutes downstream from the old trout rearing station remains – we encounter the first of 5 sets of long rapids. After this first rapids ends, there is 20 minutes of calm water, then 2 additional sets of long rapids.

2 hours 30 minutes in, we reach the 3rd bridge of the day - the Buck Lake Road Bridge. Rocks beneath the bridge challenge you. Immediately past the bridge on the right is enough of a sandy lip to pull up the boats allowing for a canoeing break.

2 hours 50 minutes in, a very large creek merges from the right, with large logs strewn throughout… 2 bends later, another large creek comes in from the right.

3 hours 45 minutes in, lies a small island on our left as we approach today's bridge #4. The river begins to change to marshland. Multiple tributaries come into view, many wide and running parallel to the main body of the river. The tributaries begin to crossover the river, at times confusing (to us, at least) the two. We soon miss a crossover to the right, straying on to a tributary path that eventually disappeared. This left us completely surrounded by a field of tall reeds.

If you have a similar experience, never fear – we were able to easily paddle through the reeds and reconnect to the main body of the Ontonagon. And it was soon just another fun memory - like turning on the TV too late to see a special that you wanted to watch, but instead find that station is running an unannounced A-Team Marathon! It was at this point that eagles appeared, entertaining us as they soared above. In reading about the area, I was fascinated to learn that, when an eagle wanders into the territory of another eagle, and the eagle defending its turf flies near, the trespassing eagle flies upside down. This is to avoid being struck on the head with the talons of the eagle protecting its home, and so that the trespassing eagle can expose its own talons (thank you to Bonnie Peacock, author of *Sylvania*).

4 hours 20 minutes in, the river incredibly widens to 150' across (temporarily) on the approach to bridge #5 – the final bridge today. Just below the water line watch for the old bridge hiding under the new bridge. There are few things more surprising on a canoe trip than skimming over a bridge while you're floating under one.

4 hours 30 minutes in, a sign announces Tamarack Creek flowing in from the right. Around the next bend, is a 50' long light rapids followed by 50' of calm water, after which you encounter a mini-waterfall - a 6" drop over the rocks and running the entire width of the river. A neat late-trip challenge!

4 hours 45 minutes in, today's trip ends at the Burned Dam Campgrounds, located on the right shore, along 300' long Mex-i-mine Falls – portage on the right. The Mex-i-mine Falls is a class 2-3 rapids. Two members (Craigo and Goobs) of our group in 1984 were, on their 3rd attempt, able to successfully run these falls when there was higher water. No such attempt was made on our 2007 trip.

Day 2 we put in immediately downstream from the Mex-i-mine Falls. 20 minutes in is a 50' run of rapids, followed by 50' of calm waters, then a 70' rapids' run.

22 minutes in is a ***wonderful 500' stretch of rapids***, ending at a grass and gravel jut out from the right shore.

40 minutes in, a large tree has fallen from the left bank. This covers the entire river except for a 5' opening on the right. There's beautiful driftwood on the downstream side of the fallen tree. Very calm waters run during the next 20 minutes, at depths of 6" to 2.5', with the same river floor gravel-reed-sand-rock mix as on day 1.

1 hour in begins a series of 4 rapids. The series begins with a 70' long run, soon followed by 3 small 30' – 40' long rapids, each separated by one bend on the river.

Mosquitoes – minimal day 1 – began as soon as we put in today at the Burned Dam Camp site, and increased in intensity up to the 1 hour point. Bring 100% Deet!

1 hour 10 minutes in, and running for a full 9 minutes, is the ***best*** (of many great) rapids runs on the trip: a very fast white water run that continued around 7 river bends. There are very short lulls near some of the bends. It's a nice S-curve run all the way through!

And, as a bonus, after the 9 minute run, the mosquitoes finally abated…
1 hour 30 minutes in is a beautiful 4 minute rapids run! While flying along as the river drops, you're bouncing like a pinball through the rock garden – this run is a real thrill!

Beware the big rock in the middle of the river where the runs ends!!!

After canoeing by an alcove and around a fallen tree, another set of light rapids caps off this fabulous stretch.

1 hour 35 minutes in is yet another great rapids run, this one goes for approximately 80'. Around the very next bend, is the last long rapids run of today's adventure, and it's a fine one, taking you through 3 bends of continuous rapids – light rapids around the first two bends, punctuated by a 150' run around the third bend.

1 hour 40 minutes in, a wide creek enters from the right, one of at least a dozen large creeks encountered today. Just beyond, a gravel finger juts out into the river.

1 hour 42 minutes in is an island, the back side of which has a small spit of sandy beach, where you can pull over and take a break.

Immediately after the island, over an 8 minute period, you canoe through 3 sets of short but challenging rapids.

1 hour 55 minutes in is a 100' long rapids – near the end of the 100', the river drops 6".

2 hours in and we reach the Interior Bridge and the end of today's trip. Adjacent to the Interior Bridge is a small, brown building about the size of a port-a-john (don't even think about it). This is a Government Stream Gauging Station. The station sign notes this is "part of a national network for obtaining water resources information… the recorded water level and corresponding rate of flow is used for hydraulic and hydrological studies."

THE TOWN: WATERSMEET

Detroit Tigers local radio affiliate: WCCY 1400AM (Houghton).

The word for this area is gorgeous! Watersmeet is located in the Ottawa National Forest. There are 10 National Forest campgrounds in the local area, among 302 lakes and 241 miles of streams, including the Ontonagon River and its tributaries. The Ontonagon drains 1,340 square miles of land – an area larger than Rhode Island. The average stream flow of the main river is 10,000 gallons per second – the peak flow is usually in April, when the melted snow pack drives the flow to over 50,000 gallons per second. Among all of this natural beauty sits Bond Falls, one of the most beautiful waterfalls in the Upper Peninsula.

An interesting piece of Watersmeet history concerns the unique logging days' connection between our take out points of both days of the suggested trip: Burned Dam (Mex-i-mine) Falls Campground and the Interior Bridge. A dam at the Mex-i-mine Falls site was in operation in the 1890s, created to impound logs – logs held by chains stretched across the Ontonagon River, and anchored to rock cribs on each shore. When the spring floods came the chains were dropped, and the logs went out in a rush, northward on the Ontonagon River to the town of Interior where a sawmill was located. In 1897, this heyday of both the dam and the town of Interior came to a sudden end as they were both destroyed that year by forest fires. What remains today? From the dam, one of the rock cribs is still visible across the Ontonagon from the Burned Dam Campground. The town of Interior has, since the great fire, remained a ghost town, marked only by a sign just up the road from Interior Bridge.

Watersmeet has gained notoriety for a reason other than the beauty of its surroundings.

In 1986, ESPN compiled a list of the top ten nicknames for high school sports teams. The "Nimrods" of Watersmeet ranked third. In the Book of Genesis, Nimrod was a "mighty hunter before the Lord." According to the Old Testament, he established a great kingdom and founded a number of important Babylonian and Assyrian cities. In 1904, Watersmeet adopted the Nimrod name as the Ottawa National Forest is prime hunting land. National attention was further drawn to the Nimrods in 2004, when ESPN began running 3 ads featuring the boys' basketball team, in an ad campaign celebrating the social and cultural importance of athletics. Each ad ended with, "Without sports, who would cheer for the Nimrods?" As the name came to mean something a bit different than it did in 1904, the school body was asked if they wanted to keep the name. Their response: "Nimrods forever!". Their principal explained, "To the kids, the only insult was being asked whether to abandon their beloved tradition."

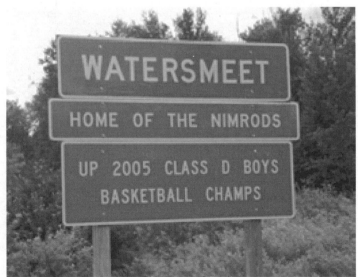

THE TAVERN: THE ROADHOUSE

The Roadhouse is located in Watersmeet at the northeast corner of the junction of Hwy 2 and Hwy 45. When we asked the barkeep if they serve Pabst in longneck bottles, he replied that the Roadhouse stopped selling beer in bottles. Why was that? On Friday and Saturday nights, too many people were using the bottles as weapons. Okay. Our stay at the Roadhouse was a brief one. The décor is basement rec room (not mine) with 2 pool tables and darts.

Sources: exploringthenorth.com, Bond Falls marker, Burned Dam Campground marker, Watersmeet School website

TWO HEARTED RIVER
TWO HEART, MICHIGAN

Level Two
Tricky

level 2
moderate ability suggested

Two Hearted River sound track:
Lumberjack Song-Monty Python
Wreck of the Edmund Fitzgerald-Gordon Lightfoot
Big Bad Leroy Brown-Jim Croce
We're Going to be Friends-White Stripes
Richard Cory-Simon and Garfunkel

Canoe livery:
North Store,
owner Larry Johnson,
18583 CR407, Newberry, Michigan 49868
Phone (906) 658-3450

THE BACKGROUND

Was the bone-rattling drive on 16 miles of washboard road worth it in order to canoe the Two Hearted? Well, despite a $200 repair bill to fix my power locks jarred out of order by the rough road, the answer is a resounding "YES!". The Two Hearted is blessed with multiple runs of light rapids, with sandy beaches on the banks as beautiful as they are numerous, concluding gorgeously flowing past sand dunes and on into majestic Lake Superior.

The well-known story is that Ernest Hemingway borrowed the romantic Two Hearted name when he was really writing about Nick Adams' adventures on Papa's beloved Fox River. Perhaps because of my own love for the Fox, and never having canoed the Two Hearted, my perception was that the Two Hearted was likely beautiful in name only. Before the first bend, I could see how very wrong that perception was, and I knew that I would want to return as soon as possible. My local car repair folks could use the business.

THE RIVER: THE TWO HEARTED

Suggested trip is a 4 hour11 mile float, putting in at the Reed and Green Bridge, taking out at the rivermouth campground – just before the river flows into Lake Superior. There are no public toilets along this stretch of the Two Hearted.

As we put in, the river is 40' wide, with enough fallen trees requiring paddling around and under to keep us on our toes. There are multiple 8' to 10' wide sandy beaches that make great pullover points. There is some bottom scraping occurring in the early going.

From 30 to 45 minutes in, we encounter constant light rapids, bottom-skimming, and tight turns – a very enjoyable 15-minute run.

53 minutes in is a beautiful (a word used very frequently on the Two Hearted) 35' long sandy beach on our left.

1 hour 10 minutes in is a long sandy beach on our left. The river along the beach is shallow with a sandy bottom – an excellent place to pull over and take a Frisbee break.

1 hour 40 minutes in, at the 4 mile mark, a very large creek – approximately 30' wide at the merger – rolls in from our right. This creek merges on a big bend in the river. Our Rainbow Lodge friends tell us this is considered the one-third mark of the trip (it was the 2/5s point for us). The extra water volume provided by the creek adds to the river's depth sufficiently to reduce bottom-skimming frequency.

1 hour 50 minutes in – 10 minutes beyond the one-third point creek – is a small island on our right. As you swing wide of the island, you're in the middle of a run of light rapids.

2 hours 10 minutes in, just after you round a bend to the left, is a 70' long gravel, sand, and reed island (Olympic Pool-sized, says Maggie). This is one bend after passing a much shorter island. Immediately beyond this 70' long island, a strong current pulls you to the

left shore – at which point the river performs its' own "catch 'n release" program, and current pull to the left shore ceases.
At the next bend on the right – another nice sandy beach. 5 minutes beyond this beach, we encounter a long island in the river's middle. Light rapids resumes.

2 hours 25 minutes in, Kenny has christened the area "Frisbee Beach". On the right is a long and deep sandy beach, fronted by a small island. The river is knee-deep, and there are no obstacles (rocks, logs, etc.) on the river floor.

2 hours 35 minutes in, yet another long sandy beach is on the left. In front of the beach is a 20' long island.

3 hours in, on the left shore, we come across a drop-dead gorgeous, 100' long, beach. This one is approximately 60' to 70' deep. Surely, this must be the most stunning one we'll see today (nope - not yet). As we draw closer to Lake Superior, dunes are viewed with increased frequency.

2 bends beyond the afore mentioned 100' long beach, on the right shore, are 50 stairs – each 6' long logs - leading up to the short-trip (1 hour long) drop off point.

One bend downstream from the stairs, we float past a 200' long island.

3 hours 30 minutes in, NOW we're at the finest beach that we'll see all day. It looks like the beach at Lake Superior (or, for someone who grew up vacationing at Grand Haven, like the beach at Lake Michigan). Located on the left shore, a good 150' long and 15' deep, just beyond a gravel island - another fabulous location at which to take a break.

3 hours 45 minutes in, a 100' long beach is on our right. 5 minutes further downstream,
you come to a "T" in the river – go left. You'll then immediately float next to the dunes, and you can hear the Lake Superior surf breaking on shore.

4 hours in, and we're at the trip's end. Exit on the right after floating below the walking bridge (reminds you of the Mother-In-Law Bridge in Croswell). This is just before the Two Hearted River flows into Lake Superior.

THE TOWN: GRAND MARAIS

Detroit Tigers local radio affiliate: WNBY 1450 AM (Newberry).

Grand Marais translates to "Big Marsh" in French, and maybe that's how it looked to the French voyageurs who named the town in the 1600s. Perhaps "Port de Refuge" would have been a more appropriate name, as Grand Marais is the only harbor of refuge that lies between Sault St. Marie and Marquette (and, some early French maps did show the area as "le Grand Mare", meaning safe harbor: in French "Mare" and "Marais" are pronounced the same, so "Marais" may have resulted from a mapmaker error).

Chippewa Indians inhabited the area for many years before the French 1600s arrival. The popularity of Grand Marais for fishing was eclipsed by logging during the 1860s to the early 1900s. The population of Grand Marais was never greater than in 1899, its peak boomtown logging year. But, by 1911, the forests had been decimated, the logging men moved on, and the railroad line linking Grand Marais to the outside world - through Seney - was closed. Grand Marais lost 90% of her 1899 population by 1915, and became almost a ghost town. Finally, also in 1915, fire destroyed most of the town's businesses.

Slowly, Grand Marais took on the appearance of today's town. In the 1920s, a gravel road was opened to Seney, and by the 1930s tourist cabins began being built. Commercial and then sport fishing were the keys in growing the town. *The Grand Marais Commercial Fishermen's Memorial* is dedicated to all commercial fishermen who worked the Great Lakes and especially those lost out of the Harbor of Grand Marais.

Today, tourism is Grand Marais' #1 employer. The area is rich in natural beauty, including Pictured Rocks, Tahquamenon Falls, Sable Falls, and Grand Sable Dunes, among many other attractions. One such tourist attraction – and a valued piece of Grand Marais' history – is the Pickle Barrel House, located next door to the Sportsman's Bar. An actual barrel 16' tall, built in 1926, this was cartoonist William Donahey's summer home for ten years, where he drew many of his Teenie Weenie cartoon stories.

THE TAVERN #1: SPORTSMAN'S RESTAURANT & BAR

The town of Two Heart has no taverns, so after canoeing we ventured 75 minutes west along Lake Superior's shoreline to the town of Grand Marais. Bud was our waiter, but not our beer, as the Sportsman's offered Pabst longnecks – always a sure sign of quality. Above the fireplace is a sign that states, "Enter as strangers, leave as friends" – based on the ten deer and two moose heads lining the walls, the sentiment is reserved more for folks than critters. All in all, the Sportsman's is a comfortable place to kick back with a beer and a sandwich.

THE TAVERN #2: DUNES SALOON

Dunes Saloon is just down the street, and is an interesting looking place – the front bar goes back to the late-1800s logging days - but a lack of Pabst Blue Ribbon longnecks tilted us towards the Sportsman's. A Dunes' story worth relating dates back to a visit a few years ago, after canoeing the Manistique River 30 miles to the south. While standing at the bar, somehow the subject turned to Canadian musicians. When Gordon Lightfoot's name came up, the barkeep chimed in: "If he walked in the door right now, I'd pop him in the mouth". Wow, why is that? "Every year around November, people keep playing Lightfoot's 'The Wreck of the Edmund Fitzgerald', over and over on the jukebox and I've had enough" (the Edmund Fitzgerald sank 11-10-75 outside the entrance to nearby Whitefish Bay). Maybe if you guys sold Pabst longnecks, people would play Roger Miller songs instead… just a thought.

Sources: www.grandmaraismichigan.com, www.exploringthenorth.com, www.translation2@paralink.com

AUSABLE RIVER, SOUTH BRANCH
ROSCOMMON, MICHIGAN

RIVER QUOTE:
MAGGIE: "THE TRIP IS A BIT LONG FOR THE NOVICE"
DOC: "BOYS, THE TRIP'S ALMOST OVER" ... CHASE AND BRANDON (THE WEARY BOYS): "LIES"

level 2,
moderate ability required

AuSable River South Branch soundtrack:
Five Feet High and Rising – Johnny Cash
Lies – Knickerbockers
Swingin' Doors (in honor of Green's
Tavern) – Merle Haggard
Can't You See – Marshall Tucker Band
Born To Be Wild – Steppenwolf

Canoe livery:
Canoe At Campbell's
owner Jim & Charlene
1112 Lake Street
Roscommon, Michigan 48653. Phone (989) 275-5810
www.canoeatcampbells.com.

THE BACKGROUND

The AuSable South Branch most often is a slow, meandering float, with an average river depth of 1' to 3'. After heavy rains – or very early in the calendar year – that depth can increase by several feet, allowing the river's degree of canoeing difficulty to vary from level 1 to, at its' most extreme, level 3. During our trip, we encountered an additional factor that can raise the river level…

Lake St. Helen is separated from the waters feeding the South Branch by a dam. The night before our float, heavy rains increased the river's depth – and the rains were so heavy that Lake St. Helen was in danger of flooding lakefront homes. To alleviate this flooding danger, the folks in charge opened the dam. The result: while lakefront homes were spared possible flooding, the South Branch – already bloated from the rains – absorbed St. Helen's overflow, increasing the river depth up to ("How high's the water Momma?") 6' high and almost doubling the river speed. On this day for our group, a normally moderate float became a wild ride.

South Branch piece of advice #1: if Campbell's owner Joe Quinlan tells you the river's running too fast for the novice, the novice shouldn't go.

Normal flow = degree of canoeing difficulty 1-2
w/ dam open = degree of canoeing difficulty 3

THE RIVER: THE AUSABLE, SOUTH BRANCH

Suggested 11 mile trip runs 4 hours through the wilderness area known as the "Mason Tract". You enter the Mason Tract at Chase Bridge and take out at Smith Bridge. George Mason made his fortune in automotive and manufacturing, and in 1955 bequeathed 1,500 acres to the people of Michigan. The DNR obtained another 1,900 acres from various sources and, along with the original 1,500 acres, created the 3,400 acre Mason Tract.

Our 4 canoes pushed off from Chase Bridge, and within the first 10 minutes canoeing through the unusually deep and fast water, 3 canoes flipped over, reflecting the plunging, roller coaster feel of the first quarter hour. The day of our float, a story in the morning *Detroit Free Press* told about Ben Carpenter, a 21-year old man who – although surviving without a scratch – crossed the highway in his wheelchair, was hit by and stuck in the grille of a semi, and then pushed for 2 miles before the unknowing truck driver pulled into the lot of his business. In the first quarter hour on the river, the part of Ben was played by our canoes, the part of the semi by the near flood-staged South Branch. Like Ben, we survived the present danger which became, by dinner time, a great story to tell.

Beyond the first 15 minutes, the river begins to widen, and people stopped leaving their canoes involuntarily. The high speed of the river was maintained throughout though, due to the high water levels, turning a 4 to 4.5 hour trip into a 2.5 hour, steady paddling trip.

South Branch piece of advice #2: if you're an experienced canoer looking for a fast thrill ride on the river, come to Campbell's after a heavy rain OR when the Lake St. Helen dam is opened. Call Jim & Charlene first to check the current conditions.

The Mason Tract cruise takes you through beautiful wilderness, incredible fishing (the AuSable South Branch is known to trout fisherman worldwide as "the Holy Waters"), and a fun look at Michigan history. Author James

Oliver Curwood (30 books published, 18 made into moves including "River's End" and "The Bear") had a log house on the river in the 1920s and then there is "Durant's Castle"…

William Durant made a fortune in the horse-drawn carriage business, before being awed when driving a Buick in 1904. Durant's investment in the Buick Motor Co. evolved into his eventual creation of General Motors. Durant loved the outdoors and the beauty of nature (his initial dislike of automobiles was due, in part, to the fact that their noise scared the animals). He found the property along the AuSable fascinating enough to make a land purchase, and in 1931 began building a 42-room mansion near the South Branch shore. Durant's $500,000 castle included 8 gables, 7 fireplaces, a 2-story tower entrance, a gym, rec room, a bar and a barber shop. Sadly, Durant's uninsured castle burned to the ground the day after its construction was completed.

Normal paddling time from the Chase Bridge put in point until reaching Durant's Castle is 1.5 hours. During the high water, we canoed from Chase to the Castle in 55 minutes. Pull over when you see the "Durant's Castle" sign on the river's left shore. After you ascend the steps leading up a hill from the landing deck, pit toilets and picnic tables at the hilltop will greet you. Also at the hilltop you'll find all that remains today of the Castle - a concrete slab next to a DNR reader board noting the Castle history.

While at the Durant Castle stop, Kenny regaled us with a little baseball history, in a story which included Pabst Blue Ribbon Beer, "the Beer that made Milwaukee Famous"…

There was a Milwaukee Braves' pitcher back on the 50s (note to those under 40 or unfamiliar with baseball history, the Braves did not move to Atlanta until 1967) named Mel Famie. Between innings, Mel would always have a PBR or two, leaving the empties littering his team's dugout. Well, one day Mel had a real hard time locating home plate, walked quite a few guys, and his team lost by 17. After the game, the other team saw the empty Pabst bottles that Mel had left in his dugout, and said, "Yep, that's the beer that made Mel Famie walk us". True story.

Back to the river. There are many leaning trees over the river that will, in the not too distant future, fall into the river and become obstacles that you will be navigating around, adding to the fun and excitement of the river. The 1'- 3' normal depth of the South Branch, with a primarily sand bottom, makes for a fine river to stop, swim, and flip the Frisbee in.

Normal paddling time from Durant's Castle to Mason Chapel is a little over 1 hour. With the high water below us, this stretch took a little over a half an hour. You will exit the river on your right. Mason Chapel, built in 1960 to commemorate George Mason, the man who bequeathed this property to the people of Michigan, has hosted weddings, baptisms, and eulogies as well as quiet meditations. Up the hill from the chapel are well-maintained outhouses for the public's use.

Minutes before Smith Bridge is Canoe Harbor, a rustic state campground.

The final stretch of this South Branch trip took us from Mason Chapel to Smith Bridge, where the South Branch merges with the AuSable mainstream. Exit on your right. The time from Mason Chapel: 1 hour normal river depth, 45 minutes in high water.

Sources: Canoe At Campbell's, Detroit Free Press, detnews.com

THE TOWN: ROSCOMMON

Detroit Tigers local radio affiliate: WKAD 93.7 FM (Cadillac).

The name Roscommon came from a sister county in Ireland, and was the officially adopted name when the area was founded in 1840. Settlers from Eastern Europe started developing the land in the mid to late 1800s, during Michigan's logging boom era. As railroad tracks connected northern Michigan with the downstate area, Roscommon was on the rail line from Grayling to Bay City – in 1872 Roscommon was "Roscommon Station", ten years before it became the Village of Roscommon.

"Tavern Of The Town" was a popular food 'n drink spot for hunters during in the 1940s through the 1960s. They'd line up outside in the evenings during deer season, waiting for a seat and a meal – as soon as one hunter finished eating, his/her seat would pass to the next hunter in line. The bar only served beer and wine, but folks recall seeing liquor bottles stashed in the back room with various customers' names on them - for emergency nips.

Today, local legend has it that, if you arrive 9:59 PM at the Roscommon Dairy Queen – 1 minute before Summer closing hour, your ice cream cone will double in size as the DQ folks begin to empty their machines. *AUTHOR'S WARNING:* This will not work if you bring friends to share in this good fortune, as the demand-supply ratio will not cooperate.

•Sources: Info MI, www.firemensmemorial.org, the Theodoroffs, Roscommon Magazine

THE TAVERN #1: CLEAR LAKE BAR & PIZZERIA

Ok, it's true that this bar is located in Clear Lake, 40 minutes from Roscommon, east of Lake St. Helen. BUT, after visiting the CLB&P, I had to make mention of the place. The Clear Lake Bar is one of those special bars where you walk in, look around, and smile. The CLB&P was packed on a Friday night–nothing extraordinary about that at a fine bar. What was extraordinary was how both waitresses and regulars bent over backwards to accommodate 8 strangers. The hired help – "Moreen?" "No, call me Mo" – was obviously extremely busy, but as fast, friendly, and good as any waitress we've ever run across. That fact that Mo brought rounds of PBR longnecks at lighting speed didn't hurt. The Clear Lake Bar has top quality food and an impressively varied menu (fried or broiled fish of several types – and white pizza… hmmm!). The locals were great – we needed a 2nd table for our dinner crowd, and at the table adjacent to our first table was a fella only eating 24 oz Busch beers. I introduced myself, explained our situation, offered to buy him a refill if he'd move to the bar – and he couldn't be nicer about it. He came back to our table an hour or so later, shook my hand, and told me that was the best beer he'd ever had – "a free one!". I'll be back.

THE TAVERN #2: GREEN'S TAVERN

The downtown Roscommon bar visited is Green's Tavern entered through Merle Haggard swingin' doors. Kinda makes your entrance a special one. Green's is old school – established back in 1934 when Hammerin' Hank Greenberg was reaching the seats at Navin Field (still can't believe that the Tigers sold Hank's contract to the Pirates in '47 – as Mister Briggs proved, rich and wise don't always play well together). Green's has table top shuffleboard on one side of the bar, a pool table on the other, to balance their lack of keeping PBR longnecks on hand. Maybe if I was a regular…

CHIPPEWA RIVER
MOUNT PLEASANT, MICHIGAN

Level One
Beginner Ability Required

level 1, beginner easy

Chippewa River soundtrack:
Baby Love – Supremes,
Dancing In The Streets – Martha Reeves and Vandellas,
Runnin' With The Devil – Van Halen,
Hurt – Johnny Cash, and
(in honor of his passing during the canoeing
weekend) *Tiny Bubbles* – Don Ho

Canoe livery:
Chippewa River Outfitters,
owners Mike Sr. and Jr.,
3763 S. Lincoln Rd, Mount Pleasant, Michigan 48858.
Phone (989) 772-5474,
www.chipoutfitters.com.

THE BACKGROUND

Six inches of early-Spring snow fell in Mount Pleasant the day before the canoe trip. Along with previous wet weather, this raised the river depth from an average of 3' to 4.5'. The day of the trip, the weather was gorgeous, changing enough to allow canoeing in bathing suits while giving light sunburns – a 24 hour "made in Michigan" weather turnaround. Canoe livery owners Mike Sr. and Jr. were very helpful throughout the pre-canoeing planning, including a post-float phone call from Mike Sr. to ensure our trip satisfaction. Chippewa canoe mates were the Father and Son team of Pat and Ryan Kennedy.

THE RIVER: THE CHIPPEWA

Suggested trip is a 3 hour, 7.5 mile float, putting in at the Deerfield County Park, and ending at the Chippewa River Outfitters. The usual gentle current speed would make the Chippewa a level 1, beginner easy, float. When the river's running high, as on our trip, the increased current speed makes it a level 1 to level 2, as well as cutting the canoeing time in half.

We found the Chippewa to be a charming river during our suggested 3 hour float. At the very beginning of this stretch, normal water levels might cause you to scrape the river bottom at isolated points, and a few slightly submerged logs could cause some trouble. Several small islands offer fine pull over spots if you wish to beach your canoe and take a break. Many small creeks merge with the river, some big enough to canoe in if side trip exploration adventures interest you. Quite a few homes sit along the riverside, some beautiful enough to move Pat to comment, "Their landscaping cost more than our two homes combined".

Approximately 2/3 rd of the way into your 3 hour float, you'll come upon the Meridian County Park, located just beyond the Meridian Bridge – pull over on your left. This is an excellent place to take a picnic break (Ryan, Pat, and I found that 1 hour and 10 minutes time passed quite fast). Meridian County Park offers a park bench, trash cans, and toilets – the only toilets you'll come across during the 3 hour Deerfield - Chippewa Outfitters trip.

30 minutes after leaving Meridian Co. Park, you'll encounter a golf course. The golf course runs along both sides of the Chippewa River, connected by 3 red bridges. Once you clear the golf course, you're 15 minutes from the trip's end. Beyond the golf course, take the left fork at the island for the most direct route to the Lincoln Raod take-out.

THE TOWN: MOUNT PLEASANT

Detroit Tigers local radio affiliate: WQBX 104.9 FM (Mt. Pleasant)

Located partially within the Isabella Indian Reservation, Mount Pleasant is home to Central Michigan University, Saginaw Chippewa Tribal Council, and the Soaring Eagle Casino. During early-19th century Tribal and US Government negotiations over the local land, a speech made by Chief Mishi-Waub-Kaikaik illustrates a key difference among Indians and Euro-Americans about land ownership – appropriate to quote in honor of the beautiful Chippewa River...

> *To control and possess the land as the White Man wishes does not make sense. Can man possess a gust of the North Wind or a measure of flowing water? Can he control a mass of clouds or a herd of moose? No. Do not mistake the truth. It is not man who owns the land; it is the land that owns the man. And we, the Anishnabeg, were placed on this land. From beginning to end it nourishes us; it quenches our thirst, it shelters us, and we follow the order of its seasons. It gives us freedom to come and go according to its nature and its extent – great freedom when the extent is large, less freedom when it is small. And when we die we are buried within the land that outlives us all. We belong to the land by birth, by need, and by affection. And no man may presume to own the land.*

- Source: Basil Johnston, *Ojibway Ceremonies,* 1990 edition p. 169-170

Central Michigan U and Eastern Michigan U's first major confrontation was not in a sports arena. Almost 100 years after the Chief's speech, the establishment of Central Michigan as a state institution faced opposition from Michigan State Normal (now called the present Eastern Michigan University) in Ypsilanti. Central's proponents said the state was badly in need of a school to train rural school teachers, while Ypsilanti stated their school already filled this need. After much debate, the state legislature decided Ypsilanti's grads went on to teach in cities in great numbers and that few taught in rural areas – and Central became a state institution in 1895.

- Source: Dr. John Cumming, *This Place Mount Pleasant*

THE TAVERN: THE GREEN SPOT

There are times that you just know a bar will be kind to you – within the first minute of our evening at the Green Spot, owner Mike buys the entire bar a drink. The Green Spot is located in Mount Pleasant at the SE corner of Mission and M20.

When we pulled into their parking lot at 430PM on a Friday, the lot was already crowded and for good reason as we soon found out. The 3 of us unanimously agreed that our food was excellent, and waitresses Katy and Sheri were on the spot whenever our beers went dry (Q: "Do you want a beer?"; A: "Is it still Friday?"). The Green Spot has a beautiful table top shuffleboard, and their jukebox selections didn't let us down. A college town bar frequented by townies and sometimes lucky travelers.

THE FLAT RIVER
SMYRNA, MICHIGAN

Degree of canoeing difficulty: level 1, beginner easy

Flat River soundtrack:
Summer In The City – Lovin' Spoonful
Do Wacka Do – Roger Miller
An Irish Song – Chad Mitchell Trio
The Captain and The Kid – Jimmy Buffett
Family Tradition – Hank Williams Jr.

Canoe livery: Double R Ranch Resort
manager Steve
4424 Whites Bridge Road, Smyrna, Michigan 48887.
Phone (616) 794-0520
www.doublerranch.com.

THE BACKGROUND

The Flat River shouts – using it's inside voice – to families and beginning canoeists alike, to come and enjoy a calm, stress- free voyage down it's slow and gentle current. It meanders pleasantly towards its eventual rendezvous with the Grand River at Lowell. There is more than just a little peacefulness to this beautiful river. With its dual appeal to families and beginners, it is the perfect place to celebrate a family event like Father's Day, so we did. With a group of fun-loving kids of all ages, including my Dad, brother-in-law Perry and his boys (my nephews) Tyler and Cam, we set sail (in a manner of speaking) on a beautiful day down the Flat River.

Please note: 20 minutes from the end of this trip lies the only stretch in which canoeing ability beyond beginner's level is required. The whitewater winds around the location of an old dam that has been removed. This is 20 minutes past the Button Road Bridge.

THE RIVER: THE FLAT

Suggested trip is a 2 hour and 20 minute, 5 mile float, putting in at the Belding City Park, and ending at the Double R Ranch Resort. The toilets at the City Park put in point will be the only ones encountered on this trip. The lone designated campgrounds are those on the Double R property, visible on the approach to our take out spot.

As the journey begins, occasional bottom-skimming occurs, the river is 70' across, and private residences dot the left shore.

10 minutes in, you float beneath a small railroad bridge, followed shortly by the M44 Bridge. Homes cease to be visible for quite some time after this point. The river depth increases to approximately 3'.

Between the 15 to 20 minute marks, you encounter 3 islands, each of which may be passed easily on either the left or the right.

1 hour in, the left shore is made up of reeds, beyond which are tall willow trees.

1 hour 40 minutes in, you float below the 2nd bridge, at Button Road. 100 yards beyond the Button Road Bridge, a beautiful creek merges from the right. Before it merges, it gently cascades down over fallen trees. Sitting above the creek, back from the Flat, is a small train trestle. This is all quite a sight!

1 hour and 45 minutes in, just beyond the Button Road Bridge, we come upon 4 stone islands. The downstream side of the islands serves as a good place to beach the canoes and take a swim break. Homes are now seen with regularity. 1' tall reeds (extending to just below the water line) and scattered stones cover most of the river's bottom. Mysterious Native American chants were heard in the distance (your guess is as good as mine).

2 hours in, whitewater appears, winding around 3 islands. At the beginning of the white water is a stone wall on your left (quite a few kids were jumping off the wall into the river), the remains of a hydroelectric dam. This is the one point on this stretch of the Flat that offers a bit of a challenge. We recommend that an experienced canoeist steer the boat through.

50' beyond the remains of the dam are stone walls, directly across from each other on opposite shores. These appear to be the ruins of an old bridge.

2 hours and 20 minutes in, is the Double R Ranch Resort take out on your right. In the 15 minutes prior to the take out spot, you'll see camping along the shore on the right.

THE TOWN: SMYRNA

Detroit Tigers local radio affiliate: WOOD 1300 AM WMAX 96.1 (Grand Rapids) .

The village of Smyrna was wilderness area in 1843 when the first settler, Calvin Smith, arrived. This likely was when the motto, "What happens in Smyrna, stays in Smyrna" first took hold, as Calvin was unlikely to rat himself out. Shortly after 1843, a grist mill was erected on Seeley Creek, a Flat River tributary, and a general store was soon built. But the grist mill's days were numbered: in 1853 the mill was swept into the Flat by a giant flood. It was soon rebuilt but burned down once again and the mill was rebuilt, and once again it burned down. The message was received and no further attempts were made to re-establish the grist mill.

In the 1880s and 1890s, logging grew the community as the wide Flat River was well suited to float cut logs downstream to saw mills nearby and towards Lowell. The town grew to the point where there were more businesses active over 100 years ago than in today's small village.

To the south of Smyrna was Whites Bridge, the oldest covered bridge in use in Michigan until destroyed by fire in 2013. As the historical marker

67

notes, "This picturesque covered bridge, one of the last of its kind in Michigan, was built in 1867 by Jared N. Brazee and J. N. Walker, builders of several covered bridges in this area. The name of the bridge derives from the White family, a prominent pioneer family. The crossing of the Flat River here was known as White's Crossing before the first primitive bridge was built. In 1840, a bridge of log corduroy construction was erected. It was replaced by this covered bridge, costing $1,700. It is the through-truss type with a gable roof. The hand-hewn trusses are sheeted over with rough pine boards. Wooden pegs and handcut square iron nails are used to secure the various parts of the bridge. White's Bridge has been in constant use since 1867, proof that it was well made."

Follow Whites Bridge Road to the south of Whites Bridge for an enjoyable drive. Once the paved section is reached, the road becomes very hilly, making dramatic roller-coaster type drops and rises (to date myself, I'll equate this with Cedar Point's "Blue Streak"). Follow Whites Bridge Road until it intersects with Sayles Road, and turn right. You'll be heading west towards Lowell. Sayles Road becomes Flat River Road. This beautiful and scenic road runs parallel to the Flat River, and gracefully follows the rivers' bends as you approach the outskirts of Lowell.

Sources: "Smyrna Bicentennial", Whites Bridge historical marker

THE TAVERN: SMYRNA BAR

The sign at the front entrance of the Smyrna Bar pretty much tells the story: "A place to sing, dance, and party" - yee ha! The Smyrna Bar is located directly one mile north of the Double R Ranch Resort. A nice, comfortable, little townie bar, with a waitresses, Raz, who takes good care of you. The Smyrna Bar is known for their thick, juicy ribs, and for serving a variety of beers on tap – including Moosehead in frosted mugs (nice after a long, hot day canoeing the Flat). Of course, since the Smyrna Bar also stocks Pabst Blue Ribbon longnecks, always a sure sign of quality, these offerings of draft beers are now plan B. Entertainment is provided by 2 pool tables, 3 pinball machines, 2 dart boards, an internet juke box, and multiple TVs to make sure that you have the right angle for the big game. Signs on the walls include, "Spank me I'm Irish" and "Beware of pickpockets and loose women", quite possibly what inspired Raz to wear her t-shirt which states, "What happens in Smyrna, stays in Smyrna".

THE HURON RIVER
YPSILANTI, MICHIGAN

**Level One
Beginner Ability Required**

Degree of canoeing difficulty: level 1, beginner easy

Huron River soundtrack:
Riverside – America, All Good People - Yes
In The Middle Of An Island – Tennessee Ernie Ford
Summer Breeze – Maitries
Sleepy Maggie – Ashley MacIsaac
Back To Ypsilanti - Lee Osler

Canoe livery: Skip's Huron River Canoe Livery
owners – Skip, Mark, and Jan McDonald
3780 Delhi Court, Ann Arbor Mi 48103,
phone (734) 769-8686
www.skipshuronrivercanoeliveryllc.com.

THE BACKGROUND

The Huron River meanders for 125 miles as it brings a piece of Up North to the folks of Southeastern Michigan. It's the good fortune of Metro Detroiters and those nearby that, whether it be a planned summer trip OR a spontaneous decision when we're blessed with a day or two of unseasonably pleasant weather, there's an unspoiled scenic river a short drive away that we can peacefully canoe downstream on.

The Huron River flow begins in the Huron Swamp northwest of Pontiac, winds through the towns of Dexter, Ann Arbor, Ypsilanti, Belleville, Flat Rock, and Rockwood as it works its way to a rendezvous with Lake Erie. When the French settled Detroit, they named the local Native Americans "Hurons", a word that they used to describe unkempt persons, knaves, ruffians, louts or wenches. Apparently, these are characteristics sought after in France, as the French settlers soon allied themselves with the Hurons in their New World battles with the English. Ah, the good old days. The Huron name soon came to be associated with the Huron River. Native Americans themselves referred to the Huron River as "Giwitatigweiasibi", which probably doesn't mean "the French are cheese-eating surrender monkeys".

THE RIVER: THE HURON

Suggested trip runs 2 hours and 30 minutes (8 miles), putting in at the Hudson Mills Metropark, northwest of Dexter, taking out at the Delhi Metropark in northwest Ann Arbor. 1 hour and 30 minutes into the trip is an excellent picnic area and home to the only restrooms on today's trip (until one bend from the end) at the Dexter Huron Metropark.

As we put in, the river is 60' to 70' wide, 1 to 2' deep, and the current runs slow. The canoeing is scenic, relaxing, and calm.

50 minutes in, you come upon a series of islands. Each of the islands may be passed on either the left or the right. 1 hour in, a large creek merges from your right.

1 hour 10 minutes in, we float beneath the first bridge on this stretch. The Dexter Cider Mill is on the right bank – if you're canoeing between late-August and mid-November, and it's a Weds-Sun between 9-5, you might want to pull your boat over for a cup of cider and a fresh doughnut. Don't finish off that cider and doughnut just yet – bring 'em back to your canoe and continue downstream, 'cause you are only 20 minutes from one of the nicest riverside picnic areas in the great state of Michigan - the Dexter Huron Metropark.

A great place to picnic – plan on it!

72

1 hour 30 minutes in, and the Dexter Huron Metropark is on your left. Easily accessed pull ups points are many, there are plenty of picnic tables, a sheltered area, and well-maintained restrooms.

Shortly after the first good Dexter Huron Metropark pull over spot, you canoe into 200 yards of light rapids. As the rapids come to an end, the river widens considerably.

1 hour 40 minutes in, you canoe beneath a railroad bridge – the 2nd bridge encountered today.

1 hour 55 minutes in, white water takes us to a rock barrier where the river drops 1'. The rock barrier and the 1' drop stretch completely across the Huron. We ran this successfully just to the right of center (our Huron River canoe trip was mid-June. Later after June, when the water level is running lower, the possibility of getting a canoe stuck on rocks at the drop off is a strong one).

2 hours in, you reach today's 3rd bridge at Zeeb Road. We float over rocks beneath the bridge, giving us a nice fast water kick for 150', before the river slows again.

2 hours 10 minutes in, we encounter back-to-back two large islands. Both islands are passable on either the left or the right. Whichever side of each island that you decide to canoe, there are fun obstacles to maneuver around or under!

2 hours 20 minutes in, you float under the 4th and final bridge on today's journey.

A view worth a detour   2 hours 25 minutes in, a large creek flows in from your left. Looking down the creek, approximately 200 yards, a beautiful stone bridge is clearly visible. This is the Huron River Drive Bridge. Looking further up the creek, beyond the stone bridge, you see the reservoir drain from Loch Alpine. Here, white water tumbles gracefully over rocks, flowing underneath a fallen log, as the creek water works its way to the stone bridge.

2 hours 30 minutes in, on your right, is the Delhi West canoe landing complete with restrooms. 1 bend beyond the Delhi West landing, the trip ends at Skip's Canoe Livery on your right.

THE TOWN: YPSILANTI

Detroit Tigers local radio affiliate: WTKA 1050 AM (Ann Arbor).

Ypsilanti - lovingly referred to by the locals as Ypsi. Before there was an Ypsilanti, a trading post was established in the general area in 1809 near the Sauk Indian Trail – now Ypsi's Michigan Avenue. Sauk Indians, trappers, and traders camped on the banks of the Huron and traveled along the Trail during their travels to Fort Detroit. In 1824, the Federal Government selected the Sauk Trail as the route of the first road between Detroit and Chicago.

By 1823, a permanent settlement east of the Huron River (near Ford Lake at Grove Road) was established by Benjamin Woodruff, incorporated into the Michigan Territory as Woodruff's Grove. In 1825, west of the Huron, the separate community of Ypsilanti was established (named after the Greek General Demetrius Ypsilanti). In 1829, Woodruff's Grove and Ypsilanti merged, keeping the latter's name.

Ypsilanti is home to Eastern Michigan University. EMU had its beginnings in 1849, when it was founded as Michigan State Normal School – a teacher training school and the first such institution outside of the original 13 colonies. MSNC was also Michigan's first tax-supported co-educational college. Today, Eastern graduates more teachers than any school in the USA. Between 1929 and 1991, the school's sports teams were known by the name Hurons and for anyone who attended EMU during that time, they are still known as Hurons. The university decided in 1991 that their teams should no longer use a Native American name to identify their teams. Huron-Wyandotte tribal elders requested, and were granted, multiple meetings with then Eastern Michigan University's President William Shelton to discuss this matter. At those meetings, tribal elders informed the President that, in the eyes of the Huron people, EMU's respectful use of the Huron name was always a point of pride for the tribe, and asked that the University honor the Huron Nation by continuing the use of the Huron name. President Shelton disregarded the elders' request, and the teams began to go by the nickname of Eagles.

In 1941, the United States produced 3 million automobiles. Over the next 3 years combined, US auto production was 1,300, total. World War II supply needs forced the country to switch manufacturing output from domestic to wartime. Detroit was the "Arsenal of Democracy", and Ypsilanti's little neighbor, Willow Run, was the Arsenal's heartbeat. In August 1941, ground was broken for construction of an airplane plant in Willow Run, with world-famous architect Albert Kahn drawing up the plans. Henry Ford's team planned an auto-style assembly line for aircraft production, with one big difference: a B-24 bomber contained 100,000 parts – a 1940 automobile, 15,000 parts.

Worker and supply shortages, lack of expertise, and lack of nearby housing for the work force meant a rough start for the venture. Finally, on October 1, 1942, the first plane was completed, "The Spirit of Ypsilanti", and Willow Run was rolling. Workers who migrated from southern states and women were added to the workforce reaching 42,000 workers at its peak. By the end of 1943, Willow Run produced

Weekend Canoeing in Michigan: "The REST of the Story"

Here's what the publisher cut off from the bottom of page 15 that ended, "Andy didn't…"

"(Andy didn't) think that it was right for grown men to have to share a beer, and bought 'em one on the house. Brings you to tears, don't it?"

BONUS INFO on "The Tavern: Andy's Seney Bar"…

Andy Stachnick, owner of Andy's Seney Bar, used to drive a big rig, transporting logs/power poles mostly, from Traverse City north to Munising, work Andy found tedious. Then one day, his guardian angel stalled Andy's truck just down the road from a bar in Seney, a bar 200' east of the Fox River and with a "For Sale" sign in front of it. Andy jumped at the opportunity to change his life, and bought the bar in 1978.

For almost 40 years, it has been the great honor of many fellow paddlers to walk through the door of Andy's Bar and be greeted with the owner's loud, "How you fellas doin'? Let me buy you a round!", the start of an evening of fun at the pub. Andy welcomed all with a warmth like those of your innards as you down a shot of Andy's favorite, George Dickel Tennessee Whisky.

Andy left us for that great bar in the sky in April of 2017. Let's raise a glass to Andy – we'll see you soon, our good friend!

365 B-24s a month. By the end of 1944, 650 a month. The importance of the plant to the war effort was underscored by FDR's wartime visit, and its size (3.5 million square ft, largest plant in the world) put in context by a quote from Charles Lindbergh, "Willow Run is the Grand Canyon of the mechanized world."

Sources: Wikipedia, www.depottown.org, www.pcsum.org, www.ypsilanti.org, *Detroit Free Press,* open letter from Chief Leaford Bearskin, www.detnews.com

TAVERN #1: SIDETRACK BAR AND GRILL

The Sidetrack Bar and Grill is located in Ypsilanti's historic Depot Town, to the east of Riverside Park. A major congregation spot for Native Americans was where the Great Sauk Trail (Michigan Avenue) crossed the Giwitatigweiasibi (Huron) River (and over a quarter century ago, a dear congregation spot for family and friends on our wedding day).

The Sidetrack has an excellent college atmosphere, with a burger that might be even better: it's rated one of the nation's 20 best burgers by GQ Magazine, and has received mention on Oprah as "The Best of the Best". The menu is wide and deep beyond burgers, including good vegetarian selections. The sign outside quotes Benjamin Franklin, "Beer is proof that God loves us and wants us to be happy". That's certainly one of the great quotes of our times. This tavern has its priorities straight: they do not carry Budweiser on tap, but they do carry ice-cold bottles of Pabst Blue Ribbon.

The tavern is a wonderful meld of history, college days, cozy, and fun. Order a burger, sit on the patio if the weather allows (or indoors in front of the fireplace if it doesn't), and enjoy!

TAVERN #2: CONOR O'NEILL'S - ANN ARBOR

A lament in one ear, maybe, but always a song in the other.
--Sean O'Casey

Conor's, on Main in Ann Arbor, is a tavern where you always feel *failte,* or welcomed. Tommy is the owner, and one of the nicest guys you'll ever meet. His staff – including Caroline, Barry, Donnie, and John— work hard to maintain that failte atmosphere. Walking through the door into Conor's, the feeling of actually being in Ireland is a real one - such as the time when a fellow sits down next to you, plays a couple of tunes on the bagpipes, smiles and walks out. How could it not have an authentic Irish feel when Conor's was designed and built in Ireland? Live Irish music, excellent Irish food (my Dad will testify to the Shepherd's Pie!), and Irish drink. While knowing well how to draw a pint of Guinness, Conor's also stocks Pabst Blue Ribbon longnecks (always a sure sign of quality) for those customers with distinctive tastes.

Conor O'Neill's Traditional Irish Pub – the clock on their wall keeps ticking down to Saint Patrick's Day – Lá Fhéile Pádraig! - one more time…

THE JORDAN RIVER
EAST JORDAN, MICHIGAN

RIVER QUOTES: KENNY'S SING-ALONG: "JANUARY, ESTUARY, JUNE, OR JULY…"

Level Two
Tricky

Degree of canoeing difficulty: level 2, moderate ability required

Jordan River soundtrack:
Dueling Banjos – Eric Weissberg
Never Let Me Down – Depeche Mode
Country Honk – Stones
Jumpin' At The Woodside – Count Basie
Parallel Universe – Red Hot Chili Peppers

Canoe livery: Jordan Valley Outfitters
owners Dan and Melanie Bennett, 311 N. Lake Street
(M66) East Jordan, Michigan 49727. Phone (231) 536-0006
www.jvoutfitters.com.

THE BACKGROUND

The first 35 minutes of the Jordan River was as much fun as I've ever had on a river. I could easily see repeating the Graves Crossing to Old State Road run several times in one day but then I might miss floating the rest of this fabulous river. Canoeing the Jordan was one of the most enjoyable experiences among a summer full of excellent canoeing adventures. This river and the surroundings are downright pretty (but that's not the reason that "Dueling Banjos" is on the soundtrack), and it maintains a fast current to go along with the noteworthy scenery. The Jordan is not one of the more popular rivers in the state since we saw no other canoeists, although that may have been due to the fact that it was an overcast Wednesday. But anyone who has had the good fortune to spend time on the Jordan will try to find a way to get back to its' magical beauty.

THE RIVER: THE JORDAN

Suggested trip runs 3 hours and 10 ½ miles - the entire negotiable length of the Jordan River, putting in at Graves Crossing, taking out at Lake Charlevoix. Along this stretch:

- we found toilets at one location: the Alba Road access, 50 minutes from the trip's end
- there are few good spots to pull your boat over for a break
- there is GREAT scenery throughout!

At the Graves Crossing Road put-in, the river ran 2' deep (after a heavy morning rain) and 35' across. There were continuous light rapids, with fun chops to them, from the moment that we put in. The initial light rapids burst - which subsides 6 minutes in – includes two spots where the river drops as if you're on a miniature roller coaster.

This is a FUN river!!!

On each bank, as on the start of the Upper Platte, there's that ole' medieval forest look: dark, damp, and severely tangled trees. It's a busy life in Camelot.

13 minutes in, there's a 100' whitewater run. 3 minutes beyond this run, a small creek (which, as we know in Michigan, rhymes with pick) rolls in from your right.

20 minutes in, a beautiful creek merges from the right shore.

27 minutes in, the river widens to 60' across while the river speed is maintained.

30 minutes in is the first good break spot: a grassy area on the left shore, 30' long and 15' deep. Immediately after the grassy area, the river tightens and its speed increases – light rapids runs for 3 bends.

35 minutes in, a gorgeous creek merges from the left, just before we travel below the bridge,where there once was a double culvert at the Old State Road access.

200' beyond the Old State Road access sits a large island, passable on either left (where there's a 10' wide gap) or the right (with a 40' wide gap). Nice home on the right bank.

The scenery is wonderful throughout the float! The Jordan is truly a wilderness river. So many tangled trees along the shorelines, you half expect a troll to emerge from the forest. Many of these trees are leaning at a 45 degree angle towards the river, on their way to becoming future obstacles to maneuver the boats around.

Beyond the island is a beautiful scene: on the right shore, a spring drops down gracefully over two of nature's steps, just before merging into the Jordan. Immediately after the spring is a tricky 80' long fast water run with the current pulling your canoe toward the fallen trees near the right shore.

45 minutes in, a wide creek – 20' at its mouth – enters the river from the right, twisting and turning over logs as it makes its way to the Jordan merger. The extra water volume added to the river noticeably slows the current's speed.

47 minutes in, a spring merges from the left. Around the very next bend, in the middle of a little light rapids run, the current pulls the canoe left toward obstacles. Be prepared.

1 hour in: over the next 20 minutes, the river surroundings turn marshy. The number of creeks and springs that merge from both banks of the river are too numerous to count. The additional water volume widens and slows the Jordan. There's a great deal of beaver activity in the area.

1-1/2 hours in: pass under the Webster Road Bridge, by its access and restroom. After passing under the bridge, the river narrows, and theq current's speed rivals that of the trip's first 35 minutes.

1 hour 45 minutes in: a very large creek, 15' wide at its mouth, merges from the left.

1 hour 53 minutes in: very unique – a tiny but LOUD spring merges from the right bank, making a sound like someone filling up a bathtub. For the next 30 minutes, we frequently see Merganser Ducks, who are quite comfortable with our presence.

2 hours 10 minutes in: we reach the Alba Road access on the right shore. There are well-maintained outhouses at this stop.

2 hours 25 minutes: float beneath the Rogers Road, by its access and restroom. This marks the end of the faster water and the start of the estuary: the wide end of the Jordan, where the current meets the tides of Lake Charlevoix. In the estuary, the Jordan widens and slows as it flows towards its end at the merger with Lake Charlevoix, 35 minutes (canoeing into a north wind) from the Rogers Road.

2 hours 50 minutes in (25 minutes into the estuary), a large eagle's nest is on your right. In the estuary, you'll be faced with options to float left or right. Each time, take the left option, always heading towards the M66 Bridge.

Once beyond the M66 Bridge, you've now left the Jordan River and entered Lake Charlevoix. Canoe straight into the Lake's waves until you are beyond the sandbar on your left. Once past the sandbar, turn left. The Lake's waves are now (for the most part) gently crashing into the right side of your canoe. Paddle to the public boat ramp take-out.

The total trip time is 3 hours.

THE TOWN: EAST JORDAN

Detroit Tigers local radio affiliate: WMKT 1270 AM (Charlevoix).

The world's largest producer of manhole covers is headquartered in East Jordan, Michigan. No, really. The manufacturer of all fire hydrants for, among other places, Detroit and Chicago is headquartered in East Jordan. We aren't lying. The company responsible for both the manhole covers (including the one in front of our Northville, Mi, post office) and fire hydrants is one in the same, the East Jordan Iron Works. The co-founder of the Iron Works (circa 1883) was 20-year old W.E. Malpass, whose energy level was underscored by the one-way 16-mile walks taken to visit his future bride.

One of East Jordan's main intersections is the corner of Water Street and Lake Street which are perfect names for a town so blessed. East Jordan sits at the end of the Jordan River estuary, where the river comes to an end as it flows into the bottom of the south arm of Lake Charlevoix.

East Jordan, despite the beauty of its surroundings, had fallen into disrepair to such a degree a few years back that it was referred to by some as "Grease Jordan". As one who had never visited the town prior to a 2007 canoe trip, I can tell you that the reasons for such a nickname are, to quote Ernie Harwell, long gone. Today's East Jordan is quaint and - as is its residents - welcoming. The local folk do a wonderful job honoring and using their history.

The major renovation taking place involves two historic buildings that have anchored the entrance to downtown since 1899.

Only Native Americans lived in the area until after the Civil War, when the government granted 40 acres in northern Michigan to any interested veteran of the Grand Army of the Republic. Indian trails commonly wound through these early (1870s) settlements. The, primarily Chippewa, tribe folks bartered and mingled comfortably with the settlers. One of the local Chippewas was known as "Old One Arm" whose nickname was acquired when he came home late one night, slept too close to the fire, and woke up with one less arm and, one would assume, a world-class hangover.

In 1883, the Ironton Ferry began operations, transporting folks across the south arm of Lake Charlevoix just north of East Jordan. In 1911, Sam Alexander was hired to run the ferry for a 2-year period. That 2-year contract was renewed again and again and again and… well, Sam operated the ferry until he retired in 1942. Sam transported so many people across the lake, that he (and the ferry) were made famous by Ripley's "Believe It Or Not." In an article that ran in major newspapers across the country, it was stated that, "In performing his job, Sam Alexander traveled 15,000 miles and was never farther than 1,000 feet from his home."

Sources: East Jordan Chamber of Commerce, Detroit Free Press, East Jordan Remembers
Melanie & Dan Bennett

THE TAVERN: THE TILTED SKILLET

The Tavern: The Tilted Skillet   Cans of Pabst, cans of Stroh's, and Rolling Rock on tap make an evening at the Tilted Skillet feel like a visit to an old friend. Originally a town house, the warmth has exuded as a bar from this location under a long string of names since the early-1900s... Fern & Holland's, Chuck's Place, Dip's, Ansted's, Sam's, & Murray's before the Murray family changed the name to the Tilted Skillet.

"Comfort food with an upscale twist, everything fresh, never frozen" was how the menu was described to us by waitress Trisha, who said the only complaint ever lodged about the bar's burgers is one the staff considered for a t-shirt, "our burgers are too fresh".
The research team tried an appetizer of hush puppies - very good. Glenn and I rated the burgers we ordered delicious, Glenn adding he's never had a better one. Overhearing our comments, Trisha noted that the Skillet's Wi-Fi password is "bestburgerever", adding she feels cheesy in saying that. Steve was very happy with his Saucy Filly Brisket. Josh said, until now, his favorite Whitefish has always been the one served at Darrow's in Mackinaw City, but the crispy & fresh Whitefish at the Tilted Skillet is the new champion. Livery co-owner Melanie added their veggie burger is the best she's ever had.

Through a sliding door in the rear of the tavern is a back patio. Here, you'llfind 8 tables for dining, drinking & socializing. From the patio is an elevated and outstanding view directly ahead of Lake Charlevoix, while to your left is visible the last few twists 'n turns of the Jordan River as it flows beneath the M66 bridge and on into Lake Charlevoix.

THE LITTLE MANISTEE RIVER
MANISTEE, MICHIGAN

Level THREE
Veteran

Degree of canoeing difficulty:
level 3, veteran ability suggested

Little Manistee River soundtrack:
Pour Me – Trick Pony, Low Places – Garth Brooks
Battle Of Evermore – Led Zeppelin
R.O.C.K. In The USA – John Mellencamp
Crazy – Patsy Cline

Canoe livery: Manistee Paddlesport Adventures
owner Ryan
231 Parkdale
Manistee, Michigan 49660
Phone (231) 233-3265
web site www.manisteepaddlesport.com.

THE BACKGROUND

In 1987, after 3" of rain had fallen the night before, our group canoed the same stretch of the Little Manistee, from 9 Mile Bridge to 6 Mile Bridge, that we had canoed for this book in 2007. In all of our years of canoeing, that 1987 adventure was the only time we've ever had to quit a canoe trip before it had ended. The 3" of rain added to an already very challenging stretch of water made the Little Manistee surge uncontrollably. Our first clue of danger was, shortly after launching, when we floated past a family sitting on shore, who replied to our greetings with, "You are gonna die". Nice. We lost all of our coolers, pads, and some of our paddles. The good news about losing paddles while canoeing a river on which you have no control over your canoes, is that paddles are useless anyway, and so, unnecessary. Warning: if the water level is running high on the LM, strongly consider canoeing this stretch at another time!

Despite our 1987 history with this river, we knew it to be a fun and challenging one, and, much to the credit of my bride, we were ready to jump in (hopefully voluntarily) again in 2007.... on our wedding anniversary date, no less.

THE RIVER: THE LITTLE MANISTEE

The suggested trip is a 2¾ hour, 4½ adventure, putting in at 9 Mile Bridge, and finishing at 6 Mile Bridge. The challenges built up as the day went on, as did the adrenaline rush. Beginners should not try this stretch without a veteran in their canoe. Large obstacles, primarily fallen trees, pose a challenge to your canoeing skills. There are no toilets or designated campgrounds between 9 Mile Bridge and 6 Mile Bridge. The recent dry conditions resulted in relatively low water for our mini-flotilla of 2 canoes and 1 kayak.

On the 9 Mile Bridge to 6 Mile Bridge run, the river's average depth ran at 1¹1/2 feet, and we experienced infrequent bottom skimming. The river width on the 9 Mile-6 Mile stretch averaged 30'. The river dropped 14' per mile between the two bridges.

2 minutes into the trip is an island. Go around on the left side, which is clogged but passable. The river does flow wider to the right of the island, but that side is also completely blocked with fallen trees.

The "dancing river" - 35 minutes into the trip, after a left river bend where fish jumped out of the water to greet us, is a nice pullover point on the right bank. I'll preface the next statements by stating that only water had been consumed to this point of the day. During this break, we were treated to our own personal light shows: the sun glistened off of the beautiful ripples of the Little Manistee in such a way that – by closing our eyes and turning heads towards the water - we viewed the equivalent of a northern light show on the inside of our eyelids. All 5 of us saw this. No, really.

40 minutes in is an island on the left side of the LM. We fought the current and went around to the island's left. Don't do this. We bottomed out on the left side. Follow the current's flow and pass on the right.

Light rapids are found throughout the 9 Mile to 6 Mile Bridge journey. These rapids are not what pose the challenge in navigating the river, but rather it's the very strong current that pushes you into the river's many obstacles on the wide side of tight bends. The life vests most valuable feature was in saving our backs from being bruised and ripped into as we squeezed under, around, and through fallen trees.

The Little Manistee's Wild Ride!
50 minutes into the trip we begin 24 consecutive bends of light rapids FUN! What starts out as a pleasant little run builds in intensity as we progress into the 24 river bends. This run features a continuous series of switchbacks that will give you quite a thrill as you pick up speed. We took close to 20 minutes of actual canoeing time to run all 24 bends. Throughout this run, Luna could feel schools of fish, 6 to 7 at a time, bouncing off the bottom of her kayak.

58 minutes in we took a break after the first 10 of the 24 bends. The sand and gravel break spot was too good to pass up, and is found

immediately on your right after an island that you can navigate on either the right or the left, but easier navigation lies to the left. The look on everyone's faces was one of exhilaration from speeding through the rapids.

1 hour in, a fallen tree was completely across the river. Today's low water allowed us a 3' limbo clearance between the tree and the river.

2 bends past the fallen tree, and 15 bends into the 24 bend run, obstacles block the river except for an opening on the far right bank. At the right bank opening, the river drops 9", at a mini-waterfall. A lagoon lies on your left, just past the 9" river drop.

Once you're past the 9" river drop, the rapids continue but decrease in intensity. On the 21st of the 24 bends, navigate around the island on the left passage.

1 hour and 10 minutes in, you'll complete the 24 bend run. It's the canoeing equivalent of a downhill ski run, complete with left-right-left-right fun turns, and the best part of the trip.

1 hour and 15 minutes in, a logjam forces you to the far right and can wedge your boat in the "V" where 2 trees meet.

1 hour and 25 minutes in, a series of S curves with light rapids resumes. 5 minutes into this, a large tangle of trees comes in from the left shore, goes almost completely across the river, leaving only a 3' wide opening to canoe through on the far right. Extremely shallow water is just beyond the opening.

A log cabin home on the left shore is your 1 hour and 30 minute landmark. At this point, the river current slows slightly, although still strong, with very light rapids maintained at a river depth of 3/4 of a foot.

1 hour and 40 minutes in is a big right-hand bend on the Little Manistee. On the left shore of this bend is a little bay, beyond which the shore is elevated 3' above the water level. The land here on the left shore appears to offer good camping possibilities, although not a posted campsite. Unseen from the river, there is a 200 yard trail from the left shore that leads to DNR-maintained campsites, without toilets, on County Line Road.

Based on all of the trees that we are scraping by and through in this section of the LM, a Michelin Man-sized life vest might be the ticket.

1 hour and 45 minutes in, a creek merges from the right bank, bordering a 60' high bluff also on the right. Within seconds is a fallen tree that is completely across the river with room to limbo beneath. 2 minutes beyond the fallen tree is a potential unposted campsite on the left shore. At the end of this site, a creek rolls in from the left.

1 hour and 50 minutes in is a fallen tree stretching from right to left bank, with a trunk sticking 1' above the water line, requiring a pullover portage.

2 hours in we come upon an island, which is navigable on its left. A 2nd island follows 7 minutes later with passage on both the right (10' opening) and extreme left (20' opening). Islands or no, the LM fast current never abates.

2 hours and 12 minutes in, a beautiful stream merges from the left bank.

2 hours and 20 minutes in, a gorgeous camp site – the best of the day - is on the right shore and runs for 3 bends. As with all potential camp sites viewed from the river today, this is not posted for camping. Within the 3 bends, towards the left bank, is a beautiful gravel and grass island, consisting of small trees and a 20' wide driftwood grouping.

2 hours and 35 minutes in is our most dangerous encounter on the river: on a right bend sits a small gravel and sand beach on the right bank. **It is important that you hug the right shore!** The danger lies on your left – at the bend. The strong current pulls you to the left where a log sits perpendicular to the left bank, and sticks 2" out of the water. Leaning over and above this log, and aimed right at your incoming boat, is a second log rising from the water to a point 2'-3' above the water. There is potential to get caught in this tangle and separated from your canoe.

2 hours and 40 minutes in, a creek merges from the right.

2 hours and 45 minutes in - 6 Mile Bridge and the end of the adventure.

THE TOWN: MANISTEE

Detroit Tigers local radio affiliate: WMLQ 97.7FM (Manistee).

The city of Manistee sits on the shore of the Big Manistee River, with Lake Michigan to its west and Manistee Lake to its east. Manistee uses their water bounty with the downtown stores following the river, and a *riverwalk* runs along the Big Manistee. The river walk features the river / harbor entrance. Manistee has maintained many of its buildings from the 1800s, well enough to earn a listing on the National Historic Register.

Many of those 1800s-era buildings supported or housed lumbering interests. Due to the cities' unique water resources, over 20 sawmills ringed Manistee Lake during the height of the 1880s lumber boom.

Before lumbering days, the earliest Manistee settlers were government employees sent to the area to run an Indian reservation (the last Indian settlement along the Big Manistee was closed in the 1960s). In 1840, Manistee County was established. The nearest justice of the peace was south in Grand Haven, 90 miles away by canoe, foot, or horseback – a distance that would ensure that the love was true.

From H.R. Page's "History Of Manistee County" (1882), "In 1867 the Circuit Court in Manistee was held in a small room called Burpee's Hall over a billiard saloon. The click of the billiard balls chimed in sweet harmony with the forensic eloquence inspired by Coke and Blackstone, while the inspiration below would sometimes become so high that the court would dispatch the sheriff to put them down. The county clerk's office was held in a small corner room just south of the bridge, and the treasurer's office was down near Canfield's store, with the funds in a safe so unsafe, that some scamp, with the aid of a knife or similar instrument, cut his way in and scooped the deposits. We next find the Circuit Court in Ellis' Hall. Then the court it was transferred to Thurber's Hall where winds whistled at the court and helped the counsel howl at the jury, while the witnesses had the truth froze out of them around the stove."

An entertaining "April Fool's Day" exchange in Manistee's early days, from an 1899 town history…

"There were jokers in those days, as well as before and since. The following is a specimen of how they did it. The first part of April, 1859, Erastus B. POTTER was keeping a general grocery near the mouth, on the north side. Jo. SMITH was running a saw mill at the outlet of the little lake. He also owned a schooner, the 'Whirlwind', I believe. In the course of the morning, POTTER sent word to SMITH that his schooner was on the beach, the men in the rigging, in great distress. Immediately the mill shut down, all hands were called and started post-haste to the beach, over the sand hills. Considerably 'blowed', the men reached the lake shore, but no wrecked schooner could be found.

"In considerable dudgeon, SMITH and crew returned to POTTER's store for an explanation. POTTER indicated by reference to the almanac that it was the first of April, and allowed that it was SMITH's treat. SMITH conceded the point, but strange to say - and this is the incredible point of the story - nothing could be found in POTTER's store available for a treat, but a barrel of eggs. By this time a crowd had assembled, and before the treat was completed the better part of a barrel of eggs had been consumed. Everybody was merry at SMITH's expense, and were about ready to depart, when POTTER signified to SMITH the amount of the egg-bill, when SMITH sympathetically referred POTTER to the almanac, with the remark that seeing that it was the first of April, he believed the eggs were already paid for, which, under the circumstances, POTTER could scarcely deny."

Sources: Michigan.org, Manistee Historical Society, History of Manistee County

THE TAVERN: RIVER STREET STATION

Located in downtown Manistee, and sitting on the Big Manistee River, you'll find River Street Station. The RSS has both indoor and outdoor seating. Indoors, the old building has a tin ceiling and a 1970s look to it. There is a dart board but no pool table. The menu is big, with some veggie items. PBR longnecks are offered, a sure sign of quality. Outdoors is a 40' x 50' deck with an ivy-covered side wall, and a nice view of the Manistee River.

THE LITTLE MUSKEGON RIVER
NEWAYGO, MICHIGAN

RIVER QUOTES:
MAGGIE: "LET THE LADIES KNOW THAT THIS IS A 3 BRUISE RIVER."

Level Two
Tricky

Degree of canoeing difficulty: level 2, to level 3.

Level THREE
Veteran

Little Muskegon River soundtrack:
My Sister Is Covered With Moles – Larry The Cable Guy,
Western Union – Five Americans,
Sugar Town – Nancy Sinatra,
Land Of 1,000 Dances – Wilson Pickett
Cool Jerk – Capitols

Canoe livery: Wisner Rents Canoes
owner Rachel Wisner
25 Water St., Newaygo, Michigan 49337
Phone (231) 652-6743
www.wisnercanoes.com.

THE BACKGROUND

The Little Muskegon was one of the most intriguing rivers on the list of 20 covered in this book. Pre-canoeing research on the LM indicated that the river is a little known gem: one of the most beautiful rivers in Michigan, but at the same time, one rarely canoed. While Wisner's services both the Muskegon River and the Little Muskegon River, 99% of their customers are put out on the Muskegon. I believe that the Muskegon is a fine and mighty river, stretching all the way from the Houghton Lake area to the Lake Michigan rivermouth in Muskegon, but I can also tell you that after canoeing the Little Muskegon, those 1 in 100 Wisner customers who paddled the LM experienced a very special treat.

Mid-May to mid-June is the ideal time of the year to canoe the Little Muskegon River. After mid-June, the river is too low to float a canoe. Even during the relatively high water of our mid-May trip, we experienced occasional stretches of wash-boarding along the river's bottom. The murky water made spotting these stretches difficult but these minor annoyances could not take away from the overall joy of the experience.

Newlyweds John Steck and Katy Fritts joined Maggie and me for the LM adventure.

THE RIVER: THE LITTLE MUSKEGON

Suggested trip is a 4 hour, 11 mile float, putting in at County Line Road (Newcosta), and ending at the Croton Pond boat launch. The Little Muskegon's degree of difficulty ranges from moderate to, at times, one that calls for a canoer of veteran ability. On the whole, beginners should look elsewhere for their canoeing fun. There are no toilets or designated campgrounds along this stretch.

The first 15 minutes features a slow, meandering current. As soon as you're beyond the 1st quarter hour, light rapids float you quite quickly past beach ball-sized rocks. Hidden obstacles begin to develop, some of which may cause momentary bottoming out, but you know very soon that this river is FUN! The light rapids come at you in long, winding, and continuous stretches.

Within the first 30 minutes, we encountered two shore-to-shore fallen trees that required hopping out of the canoes to pull the boats over and around. It should be noted here that the predominate depth of this stretch is 6" to 1' (our debarking was very safe).

45 minutes in, we reached a bend featuring a bird sanctuary: on our right an approximately 60' tall cliff dotted with hundreds of holes, each tiny enough for a bird to squeeze into, with the birds filling the sky above our boats. Multiple cliffs without bird sanctuaries, up to 80' high, are seen along the trip, often with a flat, grassy plain on the opposite bank.

At the end of the first hour, the beautiful Tamarack Creek, a body of water as wide as the Little Muskegon. rolls in from the left. A small island is the merger landmark. For the next 15 minutes after Tamarack, the river's original meandering pace resumes. Then just a quickly, the light rapids reappear, bringing speed back to the trip.

2 hours in, a long sandy beach on the right offers a fine break spot. On a smaller scale, there are many such sandy break spots throughout the trip. 2 hours and 15 minutes in, a 200 yard long island appears. We passed the island on the left and met an obstruction that ran shore-to-shore (we were able to pull our canoes over this – see photo on previous page). Possibly, passing the island on the right may be the better, unimpeded, route.

2 hours and 30 minutes into the trip, we encountered on our right the longest sandy beach of the day: a long, beautiful potential camp site with multiple pull in points. After 2 hours and 45 minutes of canoeing the LM, the light rapids portion of the trip comes to an end. The next 30 minutes of the float meanders through marshland and "no float hunting" signs. At the 3 hour and 15 minute mark, the river ends as it flows into the Little Muskegon Pond.

The Little Muskegon Pond veers to your left off of the LM River. Immediately upon entering the pond, you'll see a private boat launch on your left. Do not exit the trip here. Continue canoeing towards the bridge that separates the LM Pond from the Croton Pond. As you float under this bridge, the Croton Pond Dam will appear on your left, and the public landing – the boat launch and the end of the trip - is directly in front of you.

Time elapsed from the end of the LM River, across the 2 ponds, to the boat launch was 35minutes. The total trip time was 3 hours and 50 minutes (excluding breaks).

Of Special Interest: one-half way across the Little Muskegon Pond, sitting on the shore to your right, is a big blue and white structure with a large deck. This is the Driftwood Bar. Canoes can be pulled up on shore at the base of the Driftwood's deck, and thirsty canoers can stop in for a beverage before resuming the last 15 minutes of the trip.

THE TOWN: NEWAYGO

Detroit Tigers local radio affiliate: WBRN 1460 AM (Big Rapids) (Big Rapids).

Located 45 minutes north of Grand Rapids, where M37 meets M82, Newaygo sits on the banks of the Muskegon River. In the 1800s, the town's proximity to the big river and the area's abundance of red and white pine made it very popular with loggers as a favorite locale to cut and float the timber. Newaygo was named after Chief Naw-wa-goo, who in 1812 signed the Treaty of Saginaw, which established settlements for Europeans on Michigan tribal lands. Newaygo's existence, and that of many nearby towns, can be attributed to the establishment of the lumber industry. By 1880, Newaygo County had 26 sawmills. When lumber days were good, life in Newaygo was good.

"Sailors Pines":

By the late 1890's, nearly all of the White Pine had been cut from the area, and the attention of the lumbermen moved on to hardwoods, which grew where the majestic pines once stood. In the 1920's, area resident David Sailor became aware of an uncut stand that was not large enough to be cut during the last wave of the pine era, and he purchased the property. David cleared the hardwoods within the stand, trimmed the lower pine branches, keeping the forest floor clear and made the stand available for the public's enjoyment. David's son James has continued the maintenance of the pine stand, and today, many of the pines are over 100' tall – the ideal size that the loggers sought in the 1800's. You can see Sailors Pines on 52nd street.

In the early 1900's, Ernest Jack Sharpe recorded stories of the backwoods that he'd heard from old-timers. In later years, under the pen name "Newaygo Newt", he would write 4-line verses related to nature that would appear in the local newspapers. Here's one of his works, entitled "Where? Michigan":

Where the lakes, in emerald settings,
Reflect the skies of heaven's blue;
Where you're greeted with a handclasp,
So very firm you know it's true.

Where the bird songs seem much sweeter,
As they greet you in the morn',
Giving such a lovely feeling
You are glad that you were born.

Where the fishing is productive
And the hunting is the best;
Where people take vacations
And find joys and peaceful rest.

Where is this place like heaven,
That its wonders all relate?
Why, the place is dear, old Michigan,
America's greatest state.

THE TAVERN: SPORTSMAN'S BAR

As Katy put it, "The Sportsman's has all of my favorite things – pull tabs, Keno, and a pool table". The Sportsman's also has one of my favorites – longneck Pabst Blue Ribbons. All 4 of us found the food very good, and their 1/2 pound bar burger was excellent. The Sportsman's is a very comfortable bar. Well, the many dead critters sticking out of various parts of the bar walls may disagree. Blue collar with a primarily hunting and fishing theme, the Sportsman's is a stop well worth making

THE MUSKEGON RIVER
HOUGHTON LAKE, MICHIGAN

Level One
Beginner Ability Required

Degree of canoeing difficulty: level 1, beginner easy

Muskegon River soundtrack:
They Can't Take That Away From Me – Sarah Vaughn
Northern Exposure – David Schwartz
Memories Are Made Of This – Dean Martin
Ole Slewfoot – BR5-49
At Last – Etta James

Canoe livery:
White Birch Canoe Livery (since 1985)
owners Bob and Pat Holt
on Jeff Road 6 miles south of M55 and 4 miles
west of US27 (follow signs), Houghton Lake,
Michigan 48629. Phone (231) 328-4547,
www.whitebirchcanoe.com.

THE BACKGROUND

The Muskegon River is 230 miles long, from its Houghton Lake headwaters to the town of Muskegon, where it empties into Muskegon Lake, and is then connected by a one mile channel into Lake Michigan. Only the 260-mile long Grand River is a longer Michigan river. With the exception of some light rapids at (appropriately) Big Rapids, virtually the entire stretch of the Muskegon is well-suited for families and beginners. During the 80s and 90s, we've canoed the Muskegon out of Paris, Leota, and Houghton Lake. All 3 of these locales offer a gorgeous wilderness trip, but I believe that the trip near Houghton Lake is the most beautiful Muskegon River trip of the 3.

And the wind cried Harry…

As far as memorable characters that inhabit Muskegon River towns, we've met none that can quite compare to Leota's Harry Sanderson. Harry and his wife Love owned and operated the now defunct Love's Canoe Livery during our Muskegon River trips of '91 and '92. While taking us in his livery bus to our put in point, Harry turned down our offer of a beer, telling us "no thanks, I don't drink", when suddenly the steering column jerks, knocking the hidden Carling from his lap to the bus floor. Once that cat was out of the bag, Harry showed us how he could drink his Carling without unclenching his teeth by using the gap where his front teeth used to be (impressed nodding all around). Once off the river, Harry greeted us with huge black kettles of mac 'n cheese and polish sausage – dinner on the house, while his pavilion speakers played back-to-back AC DC and Hank Snow ("canoe livery man, he's a hillbilly fan, got 78s by Hank Snow") – an intriguing mix. Harry invited me into his house where I saw a beautiful oak dresser with 1" tall drawers, each drawer holding old 78RPM records, sitting 3 abreast side-by-side-by-side, and each in near mint condition. Harry made a liquor store run for us when the campfire bottle ran dry and seemed to think pouring motor oil on a dying bonfire was helpful and non-toxic. Sadly, Harry and Love's home – and the 78RPM dresser - burned to the ground in March '94.

THE RIVER: THE MUSKEGON

Suggested trip is a 2 and 15 minute, 6 mile hour float, from the Hi-Lo Bridge to the White Birch Livery. There are no toilets or campsites on this stretch of the river.

We put in at Turtle Pond, paddling 150' forward and slightly to our left, until we entered the Muskegon as it flowed downstream to our left. The first thought is what an absolutely stunningly beautiful setting you are in. Within the first 5 minutes we floated underneath a bridge. Trees along the shoreline bow down to the river, creating a shaded canopy for your trip. A bird symphony followed us throughout our adventure.

The meandering flow, average speed 3-4 miles per hour, is interrupted by trees that have, or nearly have, fallen into the Muskegon. This allows you to use your paddling skills to maneuver around and under trees and branches.

Adding to the wilderness feel, a good two dozen streams and creeks of various size flow into the Muskegon on this stretch, while spotted near the shore were 10 deer, 1 elk, 1 owl, and 3 beaver huts. The deer are elusive creatures and I captured zero on my camera.

1 hour and 20 minutes into the trip, high banks appear on the right shore, supporting stands of white birch giving the canoe livery its name. Homes are now frequent, some fronted with wide expanses of pink lilac trees.

15 minutes from the livery, a sign for "The Cut" appears. "The Cut" is a shift in the river created by Mother Nature, that provides a more direct path to the canoe livery versus the original direction of the river (even Mother Nature practices gerrymandering). The river splits in two as The Cut is to the right and the original path winds to the left.

THE TOWN: HOUGHTON LAKE

Detroit Tigers local radio affiliate: WKAD 93.7 FM (Cadillac).

Houghton Lake is Michigan's largest inland lake, named after the first state geologist in Michigan, Douglas Houghton, who explored the area around 1852. The community began developing around the lake during lumbering days. In 1860 alone, mills on the Muskegon River (fed from the lake) produced 75,000,000 board feet of lumber. Since the mid-1900s, Houghton Lake has been a major destination for both summer and winter fun, and is the home of "Tip Up Town", an annual winter carnival held the 3rd and 4th weekend of each January. Tip Up Town features ice fishing contests, lake snowmobiling, horseshoes on ice, live bands, and general fun. Section 3 of the by-laws of Tip Up Town USA states that "the purpose of the village on ice is to promote bigger lies, hilarity, tom foolery, and good will."

Houghton Lake is over five miles wide and eight miles long, with an average depth of 9 feet. To underscore the size of Houghton Lake, if the water was emptied out of the lake, it would cover 270 square miles to a depth of one foot.

The birth of the automotive assembly line was also the birth of the tourist industry in Houghton Lake. Once the working man could afford his freedom machine, Up North became a realistic destination. A June 8, 1914 local newspaper reported:

Four new automobiles made their appearance on our streets this week: Charles Silsby with a Ford; Homer Rutledge, H. J. DeWaele with new Auburns. With the arrival of these above cars there are 39 around town, being, nine Fords, nine Buicks, five Auburns, two Hudsons, two Lamberts, two Jacksons, two Cartercars, two Oldsmobiles, one Peerless, one Packard, one Halliday, one Reo, one Oakland, and one Galloway. Since the above has been set in type, William Coon has received a new Metz Runabout. Several cars will be added to the list before the summer is over.

The tourists mostly came to hunt and fish: in the fall and spring the lake was black with ducks, and hunters could easily shoot their limit of 25 in the morning, and again in the afternoon. Fish were being taken out by the wagon load. The lumberjacks devastation of the local forests in the 1880s and 1890s was a boon to area hunting by the 1920s and 1930s: new growth attracted deer that had never flourished because the tall pine trees shaded the ground, and little food grew beneath the spreading branches. Thousands of hunters began to plan their vacations around the first two weeks of deer season and a tradition is born.

Sources: Info MI,Houghton Lake Chamber Of Commerce, Homeowners Guide, "Looking Back" by Beulah Carman

THE TAVERN: THE NOTTINGHAM BAR

Originally located in Detroit at the corner of Warren and Nottingham, the Nottingham Bar has operated from its Houghton Lake location (on Old 27 just north of M55) for 60 years, since 1947. Since 1993, this has been our halfway stop as we head to the Upper Peninsula and the 4Day canoe trip (see "Fox" and "Manistique" chapters). In '47, the Nottingham owners and a group of Detroit-area friends – including Detroit Tiger great Harry Heilmann (see his tavern photo on page 108) purchased property in the Houghton Lake area.

The Nottingham is an absolute old-time classic bar. If you can't picture your Grandfather sitting on a bar stool here sipping a beer, you may never have met him. The Nottingham owner, until she retired in 2016, is also a classic: Virginia "Virgy" Kalis. Virgy came to Houghton Lake to stay 4 weeks with the previous bar owner and her good friend Helen and stayed 24 years. When Helen passed away a few years back, she left her house, and the Nottingham, to Virgy in her will. If you start up a conversation with Virgy, grab a beer and be ready to listen, 'cause the stories will flow… "When I joined the bowling league, they typed 'Virgin' on my bowling shirt – my friend walked by and said, 'Must be an old shirt'"… "People wonder if I'm home or at the bar – I tell 'em if they're at my house, ring the doorbell – if it takes 3 rings to get me, I'm home. If you ring 5 times and I haven't answered, I'm at the bar".

Blatz has been offered on tap at the Nottingham since they opened in Houghton Lake in '47 – over the years, one of the draws to stop here on the way Up North has been to have a shell or two of Blatz. Sadly, as of May 2007, Virgy's supplier was no longer able to provide Blatz - 6 months shy of 60 years on tap at the Nottingham. Think of this Kenny and Doc composition as "the canoer's blues"…

Six months shy of 60 years
Cigarette butts 'n empty beers
There's no more Blatz
We'll shed a tear
Six months shy of 60 years

THE PERE MARQUETTE RIVER
WALHALLA, MICHIGAN

Level Two
Tricky

Degree of canoeing difficulty: level
2, moderate ability required

Pere Marquette River soundtrack:
Hot Fun In The Summertime – Sly and The Family Stone
Take Off – McKenzie Brothers
Still There'll Be More – Procol Harum
Hungarian Dance – Brahms, Roadhouse Blues – The Doors
Gave My Love A Cherry – Steven
Bishop and Bluto Blutarsky

Canoe livery: Baldwin Canoe Rental
owner Troy Harrison
9117 S. M-37 (3 miles S of Baldwin)
Baldwin, Michigan 49304.
Phone (231) 745-4669
www.baldwincanoe.com.

THE BACKGROUND

The wonderful Pere Marquette River is known to many canoers, kayakers, and fishermen as the "PM". The Pere Marquette was Michigan's first *National Wild and Scenic River*, and in May 1978, the first river that I'd ever canoed. In addition to being a joy to canoe, the PM is a world class trout and salmon river. The river gets its name from Father Jacques Marquette, a 1600s Jesuit missionary who was well-loved by the Pottawatomi, Ottawa, and Chippewa local Indian tribes.

I've enjoyed all of the trips on the PM that I've canoed: the 2.5 hours from Bowman to Rainbow Rapids, and the 3 different one-hour floats from Rainbow to Sulak, Sulak to Upper Branch, and Upper Branch to Lower Branch. For this book, however, my favorite PM trip is also the suggested trip: 2.5 hours from Lower Branch to the Walhalla Bridge.

THE RIVER: THE PERE MARQUETTE

Suggested trip is a 2.5 hour, 8 mile float, putting in at Lower Branch Bridge along Landon Road, and taking out at the Walhalla Bridge. Baldwin Canoe Rental tells us the state may put in a landing at the Lower Branch Bridge. Until then, you'll put in by walking down a dirt path on the west side of the bridge leading to the river. As you near the water, beware of the poison ivy next to the path (stay on the dirt!). There are no public toilets along the Lower Branch–Walhalla Bridge stretch.

As we put in, and for the most part along this stretch, the PM is 2' deep and 40' wide. Be aware though, that at some of the river bends there are holes in which the river depth may be over your head. The first such over-your-head hole is 7 minutes in, and found shortly after a waterfall (with a 3' drop) merges in at a left bend.

During the first 10-15 minutes, homes dot the shoreline. As we go further in, 30' to 40' tall banks appear on the left shore.

25 minutes in, a creek merges from your left,

1 hour 5 minutes in, fallen trees lay completely across the river. We had to jump into the river and push the canoes over the trees. Johnny handled it a bit differently by throwing the trees aside (see photo on right):

1 hour 10 minutes in, the "Logmark" sign on the right shore, offers a flat, elevated surface good for taking a paddling break or throwing a line into the river.

1 hour 15 minutes in is a 50' run of very light rapids. After these rapids, a beautiful creek rolls in from the left, 5' wide at its mouth. Homes now reappear along the banks with some regularity.

114

1 hour 22 minutes in there is a very enjoyable 150' run of light rapids. This river is cookin' like Aunt Bee expecting company!

1 hour 30 minutes in, a beautiful sandy beach is on the right shore, situated on the river bend. This sits directly across from a small island that you should pass on the right.

1 hour 50 minutes in, a beautiful, dark creek cascades gently over a 4' drop of rocks. This is the first of 3 creeks or springs that merge from the right, 300' from first to last.

2 hours in, on our left, we reach the first rental cabin on the grounds of Barothy Lodge: the Eagle's Nest. Just beyond the Eagle's Nest, a pretty little creek merges from your right, dropping down over rocks next to blue flowers just before merging with the PM.

2 hours 5 minutes in, the "Barothy Lodge" sign is on the left bank, the take-out point for their guests. Leading up to the sign is a 125' light rapids run – there is a great deal of bottom-skimming through the rapids.

2 minutes beyond the "Barothy Lodge" sign lies an island that would be a great place for Ernest T. Bass to hide a still (you look at it and tell me different). The island may be passed on either the right or left however the passing is less congested on the left. 6 minutes later is a 70' run of light rapids. 2 minutes beyond the rapids, you reach the last of the Barothy cabins as a spring enters the PM from the left.

2 hours 18 minutes in, a private home on the left bank has a sign announcing that there's 30 minutes to go until the Walhalla Bridge, and the end of your trip.

2 hours 27 minutes in, a little stream merges from the right. Just beyond this stream, driftwood in the river creates a whirlpool effect in the current that has the potential to spin your canoe.

2 hours 40 minutes in, you'll float below the Walhalla Bridge. 100 yards past the bridge, take out on the left.

THE TOWN: WALHALLA

Detroit Tigers local radio affiliate: WDEE 97.3 FM (Big Rapids/Reed City).

The tiny town of Walhalla is located 20 miles east of the town of Ludington and Lake Michigan. Originally an Indian village, its first white settlement was named Merritt, and was listed as such on state maps as late as 1909. When the Pere Marquette railroad came through in 1891, its station was named Manistee Junction in order to designate a post office. The town was renamed Walhalla in 1905 by an admirer of Wagner's opera Die Valkyrie, the name Walhalla defined in Norse mythology as "the hall in which souls of heroes slain in battle were received by Odin" – but to Native Americans, Walhalla means "Haven of Rest". The man who chose the Walhalla name was Doctor Barothy.

Walhalla is probably best-known as the home of Barothy Lodge, a 320-acre resort that sits on a 7-mile stretch of the Pere Marquette River.

The history of Barothy Lodge is the history of Walhalla...

Dr. Barothy immigrated to the USA from Hungary, practiced medicine in Chicago, and in 1889 purchased 65 acres of land on the PM. This land had previously been the area's leading logging camp and had the only telephone in the county. Mineral springs found along the river gave Dr. Barothy the idea to develop a health spa on his new property – such spas were very popular at the time. In 1915, the doctor had his farmhouse remodeled into the building now known as the Main Lodge. He sent his patients there to relax, bathe in the PM, drink from the mineral springs, fish, hunt, play horseshoes, and canoe (doc, I believe that I'm coming down with something). Other buildings were soon constructed, the largest of which was the Long House, completed with the first indoor toilet north of Newaygo.

In the 1950s, the Walhalla area, the Barothy Lodge grounds in particular, attracted some very interesting gentlemen from the Chicago area. The story told of folks canoeing the Pere Marquette downstream from their cottage. As their canoe began floating by the Barothy cabins, a man appeared from between two bushes on shore, opened his coat, showed his gun and strongly suggested that they paddle by quickly. Later, the husband of the nearby cottage dwellers drove onto the Barothy grounds and was greeted by guards with sidearms drawn. These guards told him that he must leave immediately. When the intruder asked if he may first drive past the guards to the turnaround just ahead and then depart, the guards said definitely not and instead with haste put his car in reverse and drive away. Right now.

Eventually, the focus of Barothy Lodge shifted from a health retreat to recreation. The Barothy family sold the property to the current owners, the Hall family, in 1965. Today, the grounds have expanded from their original 65 acres to 320 acres, and 13 buildings were added to the Main and the Long.

Sources: Michigan Place Names, The History of Barothy Lodge

THE TAVERN:
RENDEZVOUS GRILLE & TAVERN

Located exactly 1.5 miles to the north of the Pere Marquette River's Walhalla Bridge take-out point, on the north side of US10 at its junction with Walhalla Road, you'll arrive at owner John's Rendezvous Grille and Tavern. When you're talking the Rendezvouz, you're talking about a place to relax that is only two minutes away from the end of your canoe trip. A place that carries both Pabst Blue Ribbon and Carling Black Label. A place where you can tackle you post canoeing hunger with something good from either John's grille or his pizza oven. It's a place with an owner who has a smile and a story for you. John always makes us feel welcomed at his establishment, no matter how many times that we stop to spend the afternoon retelling old stories and sipping a few beers. He has a nice dark spot in the corner that seems to be reserved for us. Nothing fancy, just good.

THE PIGEON RIVER
INDIAN RIVER, MICHIGAN

Level Two
Tricky

Degree of canoeing difficulty: level 2, moderate ability to level 3, veteran ability required.

Level THREE
Veteran

Pigeon River soundtrack:
Boris The Spider – The Who
Going In Circles – Friends Of Distinction
Living In Fast Forward – Kenny Chesney
More More More – Andrea True Connection
You Shook Me – Led Zeppelin
The Lonely Bull – Herb Alpert

Canoe livery:
Big Bear Adventures, owner Pati Anderson
4271 S. Straits Hwy., Indian River, Michigan 49749
Phone (231) 238-8181
www.bigbearadventures.com

THE BACKGROUND

It took a bit of searching to find a canoe livery that serviced the Pigeon River but we happily came upon Big Bear. Although we canoed the Pigeon very deep into the popular summer season (on August 30th), ours was only the 4th group that Big Bear had put on the Pigeon in the last year. That's too bad, because many people are missing out on experiencing an absolutely gorgeous wilderness river.

The lack of human presence contributes to two factors making up the Pigeon River float: 1) There are, especially in the early stages of the suggested trip, many fallen or severely leaning trees that must be (rarely) portaged or (frequently) paddled around or through and 2) spiders are everywhere along the river ("many, many, many – too damn many" to quote Maggie). If they ever decide to shoot a "Spiderman 4", this would be the place.

We had only one disappointment while on the Pigeon: although the river flows near the largest elk herd east of the Mississippi, we did not see one elk (we would have gladly traded a spider or two for an elk viewing). We later found out that the day before our trip marked the end of elk hunting season. The herd may have been a bit reticent to show themselves based on their most recent encounters with human beings.

Big Bear reported an 80% flip rate for Pigeon River canoeists. Our group as a whole, carried on the shoulders of one canoe, hit the 80% flip rate exactly. Lifejackets are strongly suggested for, at the very least, inexperienced canoeists and children.

It should also be noted that, particularly in the early going on this stretch of the Pigeon, shifting kids and/or dogs in the canoes create an unstable ride when leaning into tight turns, making it tough to keep the canoes upright and, interestingly, putting a strain on your back. Once both kids and dogs room to move was limited, either through placing them in the tapered front of the canoe OR wedging them between an adult's legs, the float was more stable and enjoyable.

Overall, we found floating the Pigeon to be a wonderful wilderness adventure – and one worth repeating in the near future!

THE RIVER: THE PIGEON

Suggested trip is a 4 hour, 7 mile float, putting in at Web Road/Red Bridge, and taking out at Afton Road/Cutoff Bridge. On this stretch of the river, the water level drops 9 feet per mile. The only exception is the final 45 minutes where the river drops 14 feet per mile. Fallen trees and debris are frequent on this underused river. The obstructions you encounter may differ from our experience, but you will find a fun paddling challenge.

There are no toilets between Web and Afton Roads, and only one designated campsite between the two roads: at McIntosh Landing, 35 minutes into the trip.

At Red Bridge, the river is 2' deep and 30' wide. At 2 minutes in, the river tightens to 20' wide and a white water run begins and goes with few breaks for several bends.

10 minutes in you float under a wooden foot bridge. Immediately after the bridge, the current pulls you towards the left shore. Fight the current and hug the right shore, as a fallen tree from the left shore impedes your trip. An unknown humanitarian has propped the tree up on the right, allowing space for your canoe to float under.

17 minutes in is a *limbo* tree. Take this on the far left.

20 minutes in and a challenge on back-to-back bends. To avoid obstacles do the following: on the first bend fight the current and stay right, and stay left on the very next bend.

22 minutes in, a beautiful, dark and wide creek merges from the right. Although not a designated campsite, paddling just a few feet up the creek there is room on shore for up to 6 tents.

As you approach the very next bend after the creek merger, hug the right bank. Around that bend is a large tangle of driftwood. There is a tight space to go under the tangle on the far right.

20 feet past the driftwood tangle is a fallen pine tree – this is a walk through portage.

35 minutes in, at the end of a long straightaway and to the right, are 8 railroad tie steps leading up a hill from the river. The steps take you to a camping and picnic area known as McIntosh Landing, with access to Montgomery Road.

38 minutes in, a creek rolls in from the right, 5' wide at the merger. Just past the creek, hug the left bank tightly – a large pine tree is

dipping low from the right shore. There is a small island on the left across from the tree, that you may be able to navigate around to more easily avoid the leaning pine.

Do the right – left – right – left Pigeon River Waltz, aka the Spider Shuffle…

50 minutes in, there is a fallen tree from the left shore – pass this slowly on the far right. As soon as you've cleared this first tree, grab the tree branches to hand-walk your way far left as there is now a fallen tree from the right bank. To get around the next two obstacles, you'll have to immediately go far right, and then immediately far left.

Side note: as we floated around the first fallen tree in this series of four, a spider web caught my right eye brow, AND a very large spider was hanging 1/4" from my eyeball. Not for very long though.

Once past these 4 consecutive fallen trees, the river tightens to about 15' across, taking on a very different look. The river slows and

winds, and the dirt shore lines disappear, replaced by bushes jutting into the river looking much like day 1 on the Fox River.

1 hour into the trip, the river and surrounding area grows very marshy. At the 60 minute mark, a creek merges from the left. It's very long and wide, looking like it could be canoed into for quite a distance. Around the next bend, the "Pigeon River Wildlife Nature Preserve" sign appears.

Just past the Nature

Preserve sign, a body of water at 25' wide is wider than the river itself and merges from the left. The added volume of water increases the river width to 60'.

1 hour and 5 minutes in, a 12' wide dead water creek merges from the left. 2 bends later, a fallen tree from the left shore with a 2nd fallen tree immediately behind it forces you to a 2' band along the right shore. Go in slow, bounce off the branches, right yourself, and continue on.

1 hour 10 minutes in to 1 hour 30 minutes in: 5 large creeks, each between 12' to 20' wide, merge (the 1st leads to a lagoon) left – left – right – left – left.

1 hour 34 minutes in, big creek merges from left... just beyond, hug the right shore to avoid a fallen tree from the left shore.

1 hour 38 minutes in there is complete obstruction of the river. Low water might allow you to *limbo* under the far right. There's a tree fallen from the left shore, with a tangle of driftwood in the river's middle. Our boats were successfully dragged across the tree both on the far left and the far right.

1 hour 55 minutes in, creek 7' wide from left; 1 hour 58 min in, creek 7' wide from right.

2 hours 5 minutes: fallen tree from right shore almost completely blocks the river. Pass on the extreme left. This begins a series of 4 consecutive fallen trees, one right after the other. All 4 may be paddled around.

2 hours 40 minutes in: very cool! Leaning in from the right bank is a rocking and squeaking tree. 3 minutes beyond is a large driftwood tangle on the left. Pass this through a 10' wide navigable opening on the right (the river is now 40' across).

2 hours 52 minutes in: There is a house on the hill which is white with green trim. (Go Hurons!). In the river just in front of the house, man-made rock pile extend towards the middle of the Pigeon from both banks, leaving an 8' wide mid-river gap that you can slide through. The funnel created gives your canoe a nice little push as you pass through.

2 hours 57 minutes, a beautiful white driftwood pile at the right shore blocks 1/3rd of the river.

3 hours in: you'll pass under a concrete bridge.

3 hours 10 minutes in: a 30' x 30' treed island allows passage on both right and left. There is faster water navigating left, but easier passing on the right. Immediately after this island lies a 2nd island, about 80' long with passage available on either side.

The fast water takes us home!

3 hours 15 minutes in: out of nowhere, we're pleasantly surprised by 100' long white water run, followed by driftwood 10' high just off the right bank.

Left bank house on the hill is followed by a 200' light rapids run.

3 hours 25 minutes in: 3 consecutive bends of white water.

3 hours 42 minutes in brings us a 400 yard run fun-run of white water. Just past this run, a creek merges from the right, 10' wide at its' mouth.

3 hours 48 minutes in – 12 consecutive minutes of FUN! white water takes us to the end of this stretch of the Pigeon River. 2 minutes into this run, a "15 Miles Per Hour" sign sits in front of a home on the left bank. A great deal of bottom skimming takes place during these 12 minutes – and that is with a lightly-loaded canoe. As much fun as these last few minutes are, you would not want to be on this section in low water OR with a heavily loaded canoe.

3 hours 55 minutes in: 5 minutes from the end, back-to-back islands appear in the river's middle. Each is easily passable on either right or left.

The 12 minute fun run ends at a logjam. Look left, and you can see your cars parked at the Afton Road Cutoff Bridge. This is an easy walk-around portage on the far left. Once past the logjam, exit river on the left – just before the br

THE TOWN: INDIAN RIVER

Detroit Tigers local radio affiliate: WQEZ 97.7 FM (Cheboygan)

Located 30 miles south of the Mackinaw Bridge, at the junction of I75 and M68, the town of Indian River is a major part of Northern Michigan's Inland Waterway—the unique intersection of 4 lakes, Mullett, Burt, Crooked, and Pickerel that are connected to each other by 3 rivers, Indian, Cheboygan, and Crooked. Today, this serves as a wonderful playground for vacationers. In the 1800s, the Inland Waterway was a valued and critical transportation route for loggers floating their product to mills in Cheboygan.

Indian River is home to the world's largest wooden crucifix, attracting visitors from all over the USA and around the world. The "Cross In The Woods" was built in 1954, carved from a single 55 foot tall redwood tree. A bronze 7-ton image of the crucified Jesus was raised into place in 1959.

How Uncle Ed, with a little help from his friends, saved Sacred Heart Church...

Sacred Heart Church sits in tiny Riggsville, about 15 minutes north of Indian River. In 1989 and 1990, the Diocese of Gaylord, citing declines in attendance and unavailable priests, instituted many closings of their northern Michigan churches. In 1991, the diocese turned their attention to Sacred Heart. On October 4, 1991, the local sheriff and representatives of the church were in the process of changing the locks on the doors, the first step towards the church's closing, when church member and leader of the Sacred Heart Preservation Society, Ed Socolovitch, aka Uncle Ed, had other ideas. Ed got wind of the situation and quickly arrived pushing his way in past the sheriff, two deputies, and a church business manager and began to say prayers for a long… long… long time. The sheriff hesitated arresting a man saying his prayers long enough for other church members to arrive. The round the clock vigil in 4 hour shifts lasted for 6 months! There wasn't enough room in the local jail for all 125 families fighting to keep their church open. Lutheran and Catholic parishioners fought together and through their sit-in legal action against the diocese stopped.

Epilogue: A determined group of people won at Sacred Heart. Soon after their efforts began, the diocese relented slightly and allowed Sacred Heart to stay open for weddings, funerals, and special services. On Easter Sunday 1992, one-half year into the 24 hour a day parishioners' vigil and one-half year after the attempt to change the church locks, weekly services were restored and Sacred Heart was as fully-functioning as it was before October 4, 1991. Speaking for all involved, Uncle Ed said, "With the 6,000 hours of vigil and sacrifices we've had to make, our prayers are being heard."

Sources: Mackinaw Area Visitors Bureau, Indian River Chamber Of Commerce, Detroit Free Press

THE TAVERN: THE INN BETWEEN

"Advice dispensed, cigars sold, tall tales told and leg wrestling available upon request". Steve, Bridgette, and Rose welcome you with those words to "The INN Between", which we found to be an excellent place to kick back and relax after a fun day canoeing the Pigeon. Sitting in downtown Indian River, on the south shore of the Indian River, The INN Between provides their customers fine pizza, PBR longnecks, and an outdoor deck with a great view of the river. The bar's name is due to its location, in between Mullett Lake and Burt Lake. The INN help went the extra mile to make our visit a memorable one. Bartender Kathy arranged, in less than 5 minutes from our phone call, a ride for us from our lodge to the bar, and waitress Ginger looked out for our best interests, warning us repeatedly that we didn't each need our own large pizza (thanks for trying Ginger). We ignored Ginger's warning, even AFTER another employee rescued the pie leftovers for us from the bikers on the river-level deck below us (we're not a high brow group). The only thing that you should be warned about at the INN was spelled out on a sign behind their bar, "Unattended children will be given 5 bowls of sugar, 2 kittens, and a puppy".

From our excellent overnight accommodations at the Northwoods Lodge, some of our group traveled on foot to the INN, taking advantage of a well-groomed, north-south, walking / snowmobile trail. This trail was also enjoyed during our morning walk through town, and is a part of the Indian River area experience worthy of your time.

THE PINE RIVER
WELLSTON, MICHIGAN

Level Two
Tricky

Degree of canoeing difficulty: level 2, moderate ability required

Pine River soundtrack:
I Ain't Got You – Blues Brothers
What A Wonderful World – Louis Armstrong,
Party Lights – Junior Brown
Piano Concerto 1 – Tchaikovsky
Court Of The Crimson King – King Crimson

Canoe livery
Horina Canoe Rental
owner Jim Horina
9889 M-37 (2 miles south of M-55)
Wellston, Michigan 49689.
Phone (231) 862-3470.

THE BACKGROUND

The Pine is a very fun river to canoe but has always had an undeserved reputation as the fastest river in Michigan. While the Pine is faster than average, dropping 10 feet per mile, it is a step behind such rivers as the Little Manistee and the Sturgeon. The Pine's reputation is likely due to the fact that so many more people have canoed it than many other rivers in the state. I stopped canoeing the Pine after a weekend trip in 1980 when it seemed that you could – due to the ridiculous number of canoes on the river – walk shore to shore without getting wet by taking each step in other people's canoes. Fortunately, a permit program was instituted shortly after that 1980 weekend, minimizing the overuse of this wonderful river. The Pine remains one of the most frequently canoed rivers in Michigan, and it is strongly suggested to experience the Pine outside of the busy mid-June to Labor Day time period, or on a weekday, if at all possible.

Joining me in enjoying the beauty of the Pine were the 4 Horsemen from Jacksonville – Johnny Harcourt, Keith Jonesy Jones, KB Romig, and Gomie Carroll – as well as Vid Marvin, Kenny Umphrey, Gary Mothman Muir, Colonel Braun, Perry VerMerris, Chris Wcaks, Ron Swiecki, Tommy Holbrook, and Luna and Trent Calley.

THE RIVER: THE PINE

Suggested trip runs 2 hours, 6 miles, putting in at Dobson Bridge, taking out at Peterson Bridge. On this stretch, the fast current, combined with the tight corners, has the potential to grab the front of the canoe and spin it around. Between the Dobson and the Peterson Bridges, there's one location with toilets – and it's where you'll find the only designated campsite: at the Coolwater Campground. The river is 35' wide, with depth ranging from 1.5' to over your head. The banks are 3' - 4' above the water, and shorelines are heavily forested.

25 minutes in, there is a 25' long sandy beach on the left – a good location in which to pull your boat over and take a break. Walking 30' into the woods from this sandy beach, you'll find open room for 3 tents. No phone, no pool, no pets, though.

30 minutes in, on the left shore, is the Coolwater Campground access.

48 minutes in: on private property, there is a beautiful, 120' long 3-level dirt site. This is bordered on the upstream end by a 15' wide creek, flowing into the Pine from the right.

50 minutes in – and we float under the High School Bridge. No musicals were being held.

White Water Fun!... 2 bends past the High School Bridge is a 200' white water run followed after short breaks by a 300' run, and then a 120' run.

58 minutes in: after a hard right bend, there is a 20' long sandy beach on the left bank, bordered upstream by an 80' tall cliff.

1 hour in: on the left shore sits a long, flat forest floor offering camping possibilities. A 70' light rapids run immediately follows. Just beyond the rapids run sits a 30' long sandy beach on the left shore. An oak tree stands in the middle of the beach, with a 2-tiered potential campsite behind the tree.

1 hour 8 minutes in sits an 80' high sand dune, seen at the end of a long straightaway.

1 hour 18 minutes in, a 100' light rapids run wraps around a tight left bend.

1 hour 20 minutes in, on the left shore is a gorgeous possible camp site, with a 15' wide and easy pull-up point for the boats. Just past this site is another 100' light rapids run.

1 hour 24 minutes in, choppy water with a very fun rapids run lasts 150' – and includes a *limbo* under a shore-to-shore fallen tree from the left shore.

1 hour 27 minutes in – 100' long white water run.

1 hour 30 minutes in is a beautiful rapids running through a rock garden.

Longest rapids run between the Dobson and Peterson Bridges!...
1 hour 32 minutes in, right after a 40' long island, is a churning 400' long run – sweet!!!

1 hour 35 minutes in, at a hard bend around the left bank, is a sandy/gravel lip extending from the shore, offering a nice break spot.

1 hour 37 minutes, a nice rapids run wraps itself around a left then a right bend. At this point, we begin seeing clay shelves on the river floor. On these clay shelves, the river is only 4" deep – but over your head once you step off the shelves.

1 hour 40 minutes in is an enjoyable, choppy, 2-minute light rapids run… like blowing through a straw into a glass of Vernor's.

1 hour 49 minutes: a sign announces that the Peterson Bridge is near – a sign is followed immediately by one final 70' light rapids stretch.

1 hour 50 minutes in and the Peterson Bridge landing is on the right shore.

THE TOWN: WELLSTON

Detroit Tigers local radio affiliate: WMLQ 97.7 FM (Manistee).

Wellston is located within the Manistee National Forest, and is a popular destination for anyone who loves nature. The town was named for Aldemer Wells, who in 1892 became Wellston's first postmaster. The area setting of forest, lakes, and rivers is a fabulous one, and some of its most spectacular scenery may be viewed from the M55 bridge.

Despite all of Wellston's natural beauty, its shining star may be a man-made one: the "Little Mary's Hospitality House", founded in 1982. Little Mary's was established in memory of 3-year old Mary Catherine Fischer who died in 1982 from a brain tumor. Mary's parents, inspired by their 1982 vacation with Mary and her siblings, opened the House to provide similarly wonderful vacation memories to other families with children with catastrophic, debilitating, life threatening or terminal illnesses. Families stay free in one of 6 theme-decorated apartments: Country, Fantasyland, Northern Michigan, Safari, Western, and Mexico. Included is a Rec Center with a chapel, library, game room, and reflection room for the families.

Sources: WellstonMichigan.com, InfoMI, www.littlemarys.org

THE TAVERN: THE OAK GROVE TAVERN

Horina Canoe livery owner Jim told us we'd like the Oak Grove Tavern, and he sure did us right once again.

The Oak Grove is best known for their burgers and their Mexican food and, as a bonus, it was our good fortune to stop for lunch on a Wednesday, withthe smoker working hard outside, when the special is Smoked Chicken witha side of fries. The burgers and the Smoked Chicken ("so good barbecue sauce is not needed", "can't recall ever having better") were outstanding - great fries, too. Before the burgers and chicken arrived, we were given free peanuts, told to toss the shells on the floor.The Oak Grove does food good!

The lady who held the door open for us as we entered, and made sure that we knew about the menu & today's special, is waitress Brandy.

When asked the inevitable question if she's a fine girl, Brandy said she has heard that once or twice (& that was just today) before sharing a story with us. When she was very young, her uncle would regularly sing the song "Brandy, you're a fine girl", to her. Growing up, Brandy assumed that he wrote the song for her. Shortly after her uncle died, she heard someone sing the song Brandy along with a karaoke machine, and about had a heart attack as her uncle sent her this gift from heaven.

The dollars pinned to the ceiling are donations made by customers to the "Wertz Warriors". Vic Wertz, the old Detroit Tiger, founded Wertz Warriors in 1981, with the goal of 100% funding of Michigan's Special Olympics Winter Games via a 7-day snowmobile endurance ride through Northern Michigan (Author's note: it was said that Vic's 450' fly ball in the 1954 World Series, tracked down in dead center by Willie Mays, "would've been a home run in any other park, including Yellowstone"). When we said we'd like to make a donation to the ceiling dollar bill collection, Brandy brought us a magic marker, to sign our dollars, and a thumbtack to stick the bills into the ceiling, then walked away. We thought she was going to get us a ladder, since the ceiling is too high too reach even for a person 6' tall with long arms. Instead, Brandy brought us a 50-cent piece - what? -and then gave us a lesson. She stuck the tack through George Washington's nose (ew!), then laid the 50-cent piece on the tack, before creasing & folding the dollar bill, in the shape of a bowtie, over the 50-cent piece. Brandy then did an underhand toss straight up, sticking the tack and the dollar bill into the ceiling, as the 50-cent piece fell to the floor. As Brandy said, "Come to the bar, and see the magic unfold."

THE PLATTE RIVER
HONOR, MICHIGAN

Degree of canoeing difficulty: level 2,
moderate ability to level 3, veteran ability required.

Platte River soundtrack:
I'm The Map – Dora the Explorer
You Again – Jerry Joseph
Sympathy For The Devil – Rolling Stones
1984 – Spirit, Take Five – Dave Brubeck,
Soupy Shuffle – Soupy Sales
Waiting On A Friend - Stones

Canoe livery:
Riverside Canoe Trips
owners Kyle and Kelly Orr
5042 Scenic Hwy., Honor, Michigan 49640
Phone (231) 325-5622
www.canoemichigan.com

THE BACKGROUND

Our options were two: take the more popular Lower Platte, with the slower current and larger crowds, but the plus of ending the trip as we float into Lake Michigan… OR… take the Upper Platte, reputed to drop a speedy 13' per mile, with just enough quick turns to be a bit of a challenge, and a river further reputed to flip 50% of the canoes that float her. Well, the Upper Platte it is!

Joining me on the Upper Platte were the 4 Horsemen from Jacksonville – Johnny Harcourt, Keith Jonesy Jones, KB Romig, and Gomie Carroll – along with Kenny Umphrey, Tommy Holbrook, Ron Swiecki, Chris Weaks, Vid Marvin, Nick Horbes, Glenn Isenhart, Josh Weckesser, and Steve Arnosky.

THE RIVER: THE PLATTE

Suggested trip is a 3 hour, 9 mile float, putting in at the US13 Bridge at Veteran's Memorial State Forest Campground, and taking out at Deadstream Road. There is one campground and one group of toilets along this stretch which is 45 minutes downstream at the Platte River State Forest Campground.

As we put in, we're immediately greeted with fast flowing light rapids. This river is spirited! The Upper Platte width here is 25', and the depth during out late-season trip is 6" to 9". There's a great deal of bottom-skimming in the early going.

2 minutes in is an interesting scene. From the left bank, a spring flows into the river through the open base of a tree!

Starting 7 minutes in: for a long stretch along the left shore, the land has the look of a medieval forest. It was pointed out that I'd never actually seen a medieval forest, but I imagine that this is how one would look; dark, damp, tangled, and beautiful. A camera wouldn't do it justice. If only Bill Belichick were here to videotape this...

16 minutes in: from the right shore is a fallen tree that we limbo under. Just beyond this, nature has sculpted a gorgeous piece of white driftwood which you'll maneuver to the right around. Many fallen trees challenge your canoeing skills.

19 minutes in and we float under our first bridge. At 38 minutes in, we float below the Burris Bridge.

42 minutes in is a fine break spot: a wide, dirt apron meets the river from the right shore, on to which multiple canoes can be banked. Beyond the apron, a wide path heads off into the woods.

45 minutes in: to our right, wooden steps lead up from the river to a campground (that's unmarked at river level) – the Platte River State Forest Campground. Bathroom break!

47 minutes in: as we canoe past the State Campground, the Platte current slows slightly, and flows into very pleasant marshy surroundings. There are many islands within this area and homes appear with regularity on the right shore.

55 minutes in, and we float beneath the Pioneer Road Bridge.

1 hour 5 minutes in a creek flows gracefully beneath two logs, and then on into the Platte from the right. We float past reedy islands, continuing through marsh land. Get ready to battle the current!

1 hour 10 minutes in, a fallen tree from the right shore lies almost completely across the Platte. A strong current will pull you towards the left shore, where you do not want to go. There is plenty of space to float under the tree, but you must first battle the current and stay to the current's right.

1 hour 12 minutes in a creek merges from the right shore.

1 hour 22 minutes in the bottom-skimming resumes.

1 hour 23 minutes in a beautiful creek rolls in from the left shore. But as hard as the Boys wished, the Swedish Bikini Team would not roll in with it.

1 hour 27 minutes in on the right shore, 5 homes and a trailer on well-kept grounds.

1 hour and 30 minute flow through the 2nd and 3rd culverts on today's trip Immediately beyond this culvert enjoy a short roller coaster ride as the river drops 2 feet.

1 hour 33 minutes in, trees form a canopy over the entire river, providing us with some refreshing shade.

1 hour 35 minutes in: we glide under a wooden bridge (but not of gilded splinters).

1 hour 40 minutes in: the ruins of a deck stretch out into the river, homes appear along the shore in large numbers. A flagpole on the right shore is flying underwear, looking as though they may have at one time belonged to Mister Green Jeans (by the time you've read this, the flying underwear may have been taken by river pirates or river critters).

1 hour 45 minutes in: with US 31 visible beyond the right bank, paddle below a wooden bridge, then below US31. Past US31, the river widens to 50' across with a depth of 2'

1 hour 50 minutes in, bottom-skimming resumes once again – and we canoe through the final set of dual culverts.

2 hours 3 minutes in, a creek merges from our right, 10' wide at its mouth. The river will soon turn very reedy.

2 hours and 30 minutes in: we arrive at the first of two forks in the river – go to the right (left is dead water). 1 minute later is the second fork – again, go to the right. You are now in very still water, heading upstream (against minimal current) on the North Branch of the Platte, towards the Deadstream Road take-out point.

2 hours 40 minutes in: Deadstream Road take-out, dirt walkway on your right.

THE TOWN: THE BACKGROUND OF HONOR

Detroit Tigers local radio affiliate: WCCW 1310 AM (Traverse City).

Located 25 miles southwest of Traverse City, the town of Honor resides in beautiful Benzie County, with its' 60 miles of Lake Michigan shoreline and 57 inland lakes. Besides canoeing the Platte and the nearby Betsie River, many opportunities exist to enjoy water activities in the Honor area. Sitting between Honor and the Lake Michigan shoreline, which is only 15 minutes to Honor's west, are Crystal Lake, Long Lake, Platte Lake, and Little Platte Lake.

Since 1967, Honor has hosted the "National Coho Festival", 3 days of fun including canoe races down the Platte, lawn tractor races, duck races, smoked fish judging, horseshoe contests, arts and crafts, and on and on.

A trip to Honor is well rounded out by a visit to the Cherry Bowl drive-in. Established in 1953, the drive-in's name is due to its location among the cherry orchards. When you're watching vintage cartoons on the Cherry Bowl's big screen, you may well think that it is 1953. In addition to the big screen, Putt Putt, volleyball, and the Cherry Bowl diner (with a '53 popcorn popper) makes for a FUN evening!

Local boy made good, author Bruce Catton, grew up in nearby Benzonia with Civil War veterans. Their recollections impressed Bruce with "their certainty, their values, and their faith in bravery, patriotism, freedom and the progress of the human race." So impressed that Bruce drew on these recollections for his Civil War writings: 1951's *Mr. Lincoln's Army*, 1952's *Glory Road*, and the 1954 Pulitzer Prize winner (written in '53) *A Stillness At Appomattox*. He wrote, "I think that I was always subconsciously driven by an attempt to restate that faith and to show where it was properly grounded, how it grew out of what a great many young men on both sides felt and believed and were brave enough to do."

Sources: benzie.org, Michigan Historic Site

THE TAVERN: JODI'S PLACE

Everyday is Christmas at Jodi's, based on the Christmas Tree up August 29th in the bar's corner – and what better holiday to celebrate on a daily basis! Jodi's sits about 4 miles to the east of Honor's business district on US31. Any complaints with Jodi's? Well, the "no whining" sign at the end of the bar nips that in the bud! With a pool table, multiple TV's (with the Tigers on!), pizza that is plenty satisfying – all this, along with Pabst Blue Ribbon longnecks (not only winner of the blue ribbon at the 1893 Chicago's World's Fair, but also the 2006 Gold Medal Winner at the Great American Beer Festival) – well, it's all good at Jodi's Place.

THE RIFLE RIVER
OMER, MICHIGAN

MICHIGAN'S SMALLEST CITY

Level One
Beginner Ability Required

Degree of canoeing difficulty: level 1, beginner easy

Rifle River soundtrack:
Jump Into The Fire - Nilsson
When You're Hot You're Hot – Jerry Reed
Burning Love - Elvis
Great Balls Of Fire – Jerry Lee Lewis
Jumpin' Jack Flash - Rolling Stones
Ring Of Fire – Johnny Cash

Canoe livery:
Russell Canoes, owners Bob and Leslie Russell,
146 Carrington, Omer Mi.
(989) 653-2644
www.russellcanoe.com.

THE BACKGROUND

The origin of "the Moth", aka Gary Muir, and his 1992 "Dance Of 1,000 Flames"…: It was a warm June night in 1992, in part due to a roaring bonfire built at the campsite after a fun day on the Rifle. Bill Pike - a tri-athlete - was able to successfully jump the fire and stick his landing. Gary Muir, the world's greatest salesman, also cleared the flames, but landed off balance on his heels, momentarily waved his arms frantically, before falling back into the bonfire. Fast-acting friends splashed water on Gary's sweats, helping the situation. Well-meaning friends poured Echo Springs bourbon on his sweats, inflaming (so to speak) the situation. Gary recovered, his sweats did not, and Gary's new nickname was born: "Moth", as in "a moth to a flame".

On June 18, 2005, the Rifle was the scene of "Love At The Livery" and the wedding of dear friends Gilda and Marc (Marquis) Weaks – nuptials featured with a front page photo in the 6/22/05 Arenac County Independent. Gilda and Marquis first met while canoeing the Muskegon River, so arriving in canoes to their wedding ceremony was perfectly appropriate. Early in their relationship, under circumstances explained in a variety of ways, Gilda ended up with Marquis' watch. A very symbolic event, 'cause effective June 18 '05, Marquis' time was up. The trip lineup:

Gilda Weaks, Marc Weaks, Gayle Pesek, Vid Marvin, Patti

Vassallo, Ben Davis, BK Kearns, LC Pompili, Dugal Pompili, Barb Baird, Ruggo Baird, Katy Fritts, Johnny Steck, Luna Calley, Nick DiBuono, Donna Cooper, Juan Shell, Halley Cooper, Emily Cooper, Jeanne Schwertfeger, Kenny Umphrey, Chase Schwertfeger, Brandon Lange, MagDoc

THE RIVER: CANOEING THE RIFLE

Suggested trip puts in a 2 hour float north of Omer, beginning at the Stoddard Access site and ending at Russell's Campgrounds. The 2 hours is Russell's time estimate (we have found that, if 2 hours have elapsed and, climbing an embankment, you can still see the spot where you first put your canoe in the water, the 2 hour trip can and has become 6 hours or so). There are no toilets along this stretch.

The Stoddard–Russell trip is an easy float. The current is gentle, although the higher springtime water speeds up the current, giving the river it's name. The average depth is from 1' to 3' with the only exception at the island (located 2/3rds of the way into the float) where it is ankle deep on the far right, and up to 6' deep at the Rifle's very few holes which are primarily located along the far left shore. There is an abundant amount of sandy beaches or dirt lips extending from each bank that provide break areas.

The finest break area is the previously mentioned island, located 2/3rds of the way from Stoddard to Russell's. You may paddle around either the left or right side of the isle, but the space to pull up multiple canoes and getting up to stretch will be found on the island's right side. Many sandwiches have been built, frisbees caught, and beers sipped at the island. I can smell the sun screen lotion, and see the smiles and sunshine as I type this.

The lazy man's evolution of campground dinners from cookouts to ordering pizza for delivery has been our way for many years. "Fergie's (PQ's) Pizza" in Standish is a short 7 miles away, and they have made us full and happy since the mid-90s. I would be remiss if I did not mention the dinner time carry-out wonder of Omer's own "Ma's Girls Cafe's" pan fried perch and chicken.

THE TOWN: OMER

Detroit Tigers local radio affiliate: WSGW 790AM (Saginaw).

Omer welcomes you with a sign that declares it is "the smallest city in Michigan". As the same commercial is playing on your car radio when you leave town as when you had hit town, you have little reason to doubt the claim. Main Street sits on US23, 7 miles north of Standish, 30 miles above Bay City. "Ma's Girls Cafe", formerly Ziggy's Diner, provides an excellent breakfast before hitting the day's canoeing. Tradition dictates post-breakfast wandering from Ma's to the flea market that shares the same parking lot.

Founded in 1866 as Rifle River Mills, the name was changed to Homer 6 years later in honor of one of the town's founding fathers, Frank Homer. When state maps became popular in Homer, someone noticed that Michigan already had a Homer. Using the bare minimum of creativity, town elders dropped the H and Omer was born. Once the road to Standish was completed, Omer began to see stage coaches arrive and business flourish.

BUT then... well, think of the King of Swamp Castle from Monty Python's Holy Grail
"When I first came here, this was all swamp. Everyone said I was daft to build a castle on a swamp, but I built it all the same, just to show them. It sank into the swamp. So I built a second one. That sank into the swamp. So I built a third. That burned down, fell over, then sank into the swamp. But the fourth one stayed up. And that's what you're going to get, Lad, the strongest castle in all of England"...

* 1881 a fire burned Omer to the ground – they rebuilt
* 1900 a tornado leveled Omer – they rebuilt
* 1903 a 2nd fire burned down Omer's business section – they rebuilt
* 1914 fire engulfed the entire city, picking up force when it reached the hardware store, exploding the 400 pounds of dynamite kept there, destroying every remaining business in the town – and again they rebuilt
* 1916 winter snows and spring rains caused the Rifle to flood, destroying the dam and the water system. The entire town was covered with debris, sand, and silt. This 35 year run got quite a few folks heading for safer locales, but the ones who stayed rebuilt Omer and the town you see today. Knock on wood.

Sources: Ziggy's place mat; Monty Python's Holy Grail

THE TAVERN: THE HAT BAR & RUSSELL'S CAMPGROUND

Depart the grounds of Russell's Canoes at US23 and, if you wished to visit the Hat Bar, you would've turned right and it's 500 feet away until May of 2007 when their doors closed for the last time. The bar's name came from the hats that used to smokily hang from the tavern's ceiling. With the passing of the Hat Bar, the final Omer bar has passed on. Fortunately for all, Russell's Campground has served as a wonderful party location after the canoeing since 1986, and as the home of the aforementioned "Love At The Livery" wedding and reception! Once off of the river, should you not want to cookout, your food for the night is covered by deliveries from either PQ's (Standish) or Ma's Girls (Omer) right to where you, your hunger, your chair, and your cooler await.

THE STURGEON RIVER
WOLVERINE, MICHIGAN

Level THREE
Veteran

Degree of canoeing difficulty: level
3, veteran ability suggested

Sturgeon River soundtrack:
Rodeo Song – Gary Lee
Bottle Of Wine – The Fireballs
Movin' On Over – Hank Williams
Family Tradition – Hank Jr.
Wooly Bully - Sam the Sham and The Pharaohs

Canoe livery:
Sturgeon River Paddlesports
Owners Jamie & Meghan
12961 S. Straits Hwy., Wolverine, Michigan 49799.
Phone (231) 525-6878
www.sturgeonriverpaddle.com.

THE BACKGROUND

The Sturgeon River has been touted as the fastest flow in the Lower Peninsula (it gets my vote!) and a Blue Ribbon trout stream (I'm not a fisherman, but any reference to a cold Pabst Beer works for me – and some awfully large fish did swim by our boats). The Sturgeon current was very fast during our entire trip, due to the advertised fact that the river has an average descent of 14' per mile. The Sturgeon also has this unique feature: while the middle 3/4ths of the river is a very fast downstream flow, in many points a band of water 2'-3' wide along each shore is actually flowing upstream! As a result, on some of the tight turns, if your canoe gets too close to shore where the conflicting currents meet you have to fight a whirlpool effect to avoid having your boat spun in a circle. Based on how engaged both our front and rear canoeists were in navigating the Sturgeon I believe that a solo canoeist would have difficulties at times in keeping his or her boat facing downstream.

THE RIVER: THE STURGEON

Suggested trip is a 2 hour, 6 mile float, putting in at Wolverine Park, a short walk from the historic Wolverine Train Station and taking out at the Rondo DNR site.

The river current moved our canoes quickly as soon as we shoved off. The width of the river here is approximately 15' wide and doesn't vary a great deal from a width of 15' to 25' the balance of the suggested trip. Long straight-aways vs. tight bends predominate.

25 minutes from Wolverine Park, on the right bank of the Sturgeon, you'll come upon DNR outhouses that are the only toilets along this stretch of the river.

30 minutes from Wolverine Park is Scott Bridge. There is a sudden 3' river level drop just beyond the bridge, along with a good amount of white water. Cut back hard left once you've passed under the bridge.

It was just after the 3' drop that we first noticed the whirlpool action previously noted: if you do not cut back hard left, you'll be pulled into the right shore and spun so that you're facing upstream (due to the fast downstream middle current meeting the 2' – 3' band along the shore of water moving upstream).

10 minutes downstream from Scott Bridge, look to your left and you'll see another wonder of canoeing the Sturgeon –a bar sitting about 100 yards away. This is not a mirage, but rather the Thirsty Sturgeon formerly Meadow's Bar.

After our break at the Thirsty Sturgeon, we're back on the Sturgeon River, fat and happy. From Thirsty Sturgeon's to the end of the trip at the Rondo DNR launch site, 1 hour and 15 minutes of canoeing time remain.

The fast current and white water are maintained for the balance of the trip. The whirlpools increase in frequency the nearer you get to the take out point, as the river steps up its efforts to spin the front of the canoe around. Long stretches of white water slow down at the bends allowing you the option of taking a canoe break, walking upstream next to shore (where the water moves upstream with you), and jumping in the middle current without your boat for a 100' – 150' white water float with a soft landing at the bend.

Homes appear with more frequency in the back half of the Sturgeon. The Rondo DNR launch and the trip's end will be on your left, just beyond the bridge.

THE TOWN: WOLVERINE

Detroit Tigers local radio affiliate: WQEZ 97.7 FM (Cheboygan).

Wolverine is located in southwestern Cheboygan County, 1 mile west of I75 and 35 miles south of the Mackinac Bridge. The Sturgeon River is a very popular fishing as well as canoeing spot and flows through the town of Wolverine. Our suggested trip put-in point is only 200 yards from the train depot. The Wolverine Train Depot is a registered "Michigan Historic Site", as noted by the sign in front of the building.

There are a great deal of resorts in Wolverine and the surrounding area. We chose to stay in Malone's Cabins for our lodging, and we were glad that we did. Malone's 4 cabins sit just south of town on the east side of Old 27. Tightly packed Hemlock trees above the cabins provides natural air conditioning that you feel as soon as you enter your unit. A short 20' outside the back door of each cabin, the West Branch of the Sturgeon flows, running parallel with the cabins. After a fun day on the Sturgeon, relaxing on your back porch chair watching the West Branch of the river flow by is a beautiful conclusion to a great day.

Wolverine began its growth during the lumber boom of the 1880s. The Michigan Central Railroad, responding to the demand of the logging explosion, built the train station in 1881. The town, originally named Torrey in 1881, was renamed Wolverine in 1882 after the state animal, abundant in the region at that time. Surprisingly, after the logging days subsided in the early 1900s, the Wolverine train schedule actually increased in volume. The reason for this was the spike in tourists to the Mackinac Straits, as the MCRR (Michigan Central Railroad) began promoting Northern Michigan as "curative of hay fever, asthma, bronchial and lung affections."

Sources: Bureau of History - Michigan Dept. of State; Info MI

THE TAVERN #1: THIRSTY STURGEON

The location alone,100 yards off of the river, with a friendly place to pull the boats ashore and a short walk across a flat, grassy plain, combine to make the Thirsty Sturgeon, the old Meadows Bar, a fine place to take a paddling break. The burgers and sandwiches are excellent and our 4 canoers said the pizza immediately makes the bar a destination stop on subsequent Up North trips. Pabst Blue Ribbon longnecks are on hand as the perfect accompaniment to the pizza. A pool table and a juke box round out your Thirsty Sturgeon experience.

THE TAVERN #2: VICKIE J'S BAR

The sign outside was like a magnet to us: "Home Of the 3" Burgers". Vickie J's is a wonderful little tavern and about the size of your living room. Bar features include restroom signs "inboard" and "outboard", an excellent juke box to lay down your soundtrack for the night, and a pool table is there for you, too. As with all outstanding establishments, chilled PBR longnecks are available. Our waitress, Dee, made us feel right at home. Vickie J's Bar is on Old 27, 1 mile south of Wolverine. My Grandpa would be here if he could.

THE WHITE RIVER
MONTAGUE, MICHIGAN

**Level One
Beginner Ability Required**

Degree of canoeing difficulty: level 1, beginner easy... to level 2, moderate ability required

**Level Two
Tricky**

White River soundtrack:
Messin' With The Kid – Junior Wells
Moonbeam Song – Nilsson
Talkin' At The Texaco – James McMurtry
Small Town – John Mellencamp
Who Stole My Keeshaka? – Maty Brothers

Canoe livery:
Happy Mohawk Canoe Livery
owners Dave and Jill Cordray
735 Fruitvale , Montague, Michigan 49437.
Ph. (231) 894-4209
www.happymohawkcanoelivery.com.

THE BACKGROUND

From 1974 to 1992, my family owned a cottage on nearby Lake Michigan. During many of those summers, we took a canoe trip down the White River with the folks at Happy Mohawk. We always floated the same stretch, from the Twin Rollway to the livery office. I considered that portion of the White to be the finest section of river anywhere in the state for taking Frisbee throwing breaks: slow current, knee-deep water, complete with a sandy bottom free of large rocks and hidden obstacleswhich made it a kind-to-your- body Frisbee diving river. The Twin Rollway put in point was closed by the state in the late-80s. Isn't it amazing how often, when we're forced out of a favorite ritual, a wonderful surprise is the result.

With the Twin Rollway entry closed, we chose to float from the livery, our old end point, to the Old Trading Post Landing advertised as a 3 hour, 7 mile trip. 10 minutes into this stretch, and running for 40 minutes, begins a series of "spreads" in the river. While not as tight shore-to-shore as the Upper Peninsula's Fox River spreads, nor as fast, the White River spreads were still quite a treat. At the 10 minute in mark, the river divides and then divides again, coming back to one solid waterway 40 minutes later. Happy Mohawk employees suggested that we stay to the right through the spreads, but we had found that you can chose to take either the left OR right split at any of the many options, separate yourself from fellow canoers, and come back to the same main body of water downstream.

THE RIVER: THE WHITE

The suggested trip begins at the Happy Mohawk livery on Fruitvale Road, finishing at the Old Trading Post Landing, a trip that took us 2 and a half hours to canoe. Toilets are found on this stretch at the White River Campground, just over 1 hour downstream from the Happy Mohawk.

Within the first 5 minutes of the trip, creeks merge from the right and then the left. The White is running 1' to 1-1/2' deep and is 40' wide. You come across many fallen trees in the first few minutes of the voyage, blocking between 1/4 to 2/3 of the river width. At 10 minutes in, a creek flows in from the left, widening the river briefly to 60' across. This marks the beginning of the previously mentioned "spreads".

The White River Spreads: within the first 10 minutes of hitting the spreads (ie, between 10 minutes to 20 minutes into the trip), the river presents you with 5 options to either float to the left or to the right. The river will split again and again over the 40 minutes of the spreads. Whether you choose left or right at each option, you'll eventually come back to the river's main body. At one point in the midst of the spreads, we came up to a busy aquatic intersection where we were presented the options of floating left, right, or plunge right up the middle – a visual delight! The river width – 60' at the start of the spreads – tightens to 20'–30' within the spreads.

25 minutes downstream from the livery, a small creek merges from the left as you float around a right bend. The right bend offers a small sandy lip that you can pull your boat ashore and take a break. 100' past this bend is an island that you may pass on either the left or right.

30 minutes in, a large island in the middle of the river may be passed either left or right, but is more navigable on the left.

32 minutes in is a section of the spreads where 4 waterways form a junction in the middle of the river. This 4-waterway intersection repeats itself in 5 minutes. Very fun!

50 minutes in, the 11th and final river split has been encountered within the spreads.

From the 55 minute mark to the 1 hour mark, 3 creeks roll in from your left. The third creek is the largest, 20' wide at it's merger with the White River.

White River Campground: reached on the right shore, 1 hour and 5 minutes into the trip. A large sign, on the river's right bank before the campground, announces "10 minutes to the WRC" and "1 ½ hours to the Old Trading Post". The White River Campground is big, with 235 campsites, and is a fine restroom break spot.

3-5 minutes downstream from the campground, a creek flows in from the left, then the right, just before an island. At the island, you'll see two large arrows that direct you to the right of the island. The first arrow is on a tree that blocks access to the island's left side… the 2nd arrow is on a tree to the right of the first arrow. Heed the arrows!

1 hour 15 minutes in, a creek flows in from the right, 12'-15' wide at the merger.

1 hour 20 minutes in, the river width tightens to 15' across as you float through several S curves. Within the S curves, a lagoon feeds the river from the right shore.

1 hour 25 minutes in, a baby creek with several logs across it, rolls in from the right. 2 minutes later is a 50' long island on your left. We begin to encounter occasional bottom skimming that will be with us until the end of the trip.

1 hour 40 minutes in, a river split may be taken to either the left or the right, but is more navigable on the right.

1 hour 45 minutes in is a creek on the right, 18'-20' wide at the river merger.

1 hour 50 minutes in, 2 waterways merge from the left, 20' apart going around a small island

1 hour 55 minutes in, a large waterway merges from the left, 25' wide at the mouth.

2 hours in, a fallen tree from the right shore blocks the river, except for a 15' opening on the left. Approach slowly as the current pulls your canoe towards the middle of the tree, then cutback hard left to shoot the opening. This is immediately follows by a big creek merging from the left.

2 hours 15 minutes in, a creek merges from the right.

2 hours 20 minutes in, pass the island on the right.

2 hours 25 minutes in is a large creek merging from your left – 5 minutes to go!

2 hours 30 minutes in, the trip ends at the Old Trading Post Landing, on your right.

THE TOWN: MONTAGUE

Detroit Tigers local radio affiliate: WOOD 106.9 FM (Muskegon).

Montague is situated on the north of White Lake, on high ground overlooking the White River Channel and Montague's sister city of Whitehall.

In the 1840s, this general area was home to the great Indian Chief Owasippe. The chief had two sons who, one day, went down to fish on the White River and never returned. Owasippe sat for hours each day on a high bluff looking down over the White River, waiting in vain for his sons' return. Shortly after the great chief's death, two canoes with a skeleton in each were found under a river bank which had caved in, killing his sons. The large pine tree that Chief Owasippe died under is today known as "Burying Ground Point".

Modern Montague can trace its roots to the War of 1812. A veteran of the war, Job Sargent, was given a very large land grant in the Michigan Territory to homestead as a reward for service to his country. That land grant made up much of what today is Montague. In 1855, Job's son Nat built Montague's first home and first blacksmith shop.

In 1861, William Ferry laid out plans for a village to be known as "Montague", which not so coincidentally, was William's middle name. The street on which Jimmy's Tavern and Lipka's Old Fashion Soda Fountain both sit is named Ferry Street, William's last name. If William were alive today, it can be assumed that he could make an excellent living advising Presidents on how to establish a lasting legacy.

By 1881, the lumber boom was at its peak in the Montague area. All 28 lumber mills were in business around White Lake. The riches were flowing and the local lumber barons used a portion of the money to build a fairgrounds. The fairgrounds were very popular with the common folk for the many fairs they enjoyed over the next 24 years. The lumber barons enjoyed the grounds for a different reason: the many horse races that they staged on the grounds. In 1905, once all of the local timber had been ravaged by the rich men, the fairs stopped and the buildings on the grounds were torn down. The good news is that 1905 was the year Tyrus Raymond Cobb joined the Detroit Tigers. It's all about balance.

Today, the Montague economy is supported primarily by tourism. The same riches of water that attracted the lumber men now attract vacationers. For those people trying to find the town, just look for the world's largest weathervane.

Sources: The White Lake Area Historical Society pamphlet, Info MI.

THE TAVERN: JIMMY'S TAVERN

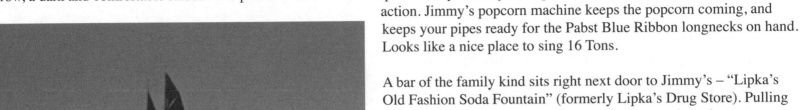

Jimmy's Tavern, located on Ferry Street in Montague, has recovered quite nicely – thank you - from a 1990's fire. Jimmy's is long and narrow, a dark and comfortable saloon. The patrons and the hired help were very friendly during our visit. Two pool tables are ready for action. Jimmy's popcorn machine keeps the popcorn coming, and keeps your pipes ready for the Pabst Blue Ribbon longnecks on hand. Looks like a nice place to sing 16 Tons.

A bar of the family kind sits right next door to Jimmy's – "Lipka's Old Fashion Soda Fountain" (formerly Lipka's Drug Store). Pulling up a bar stool at Lipka's won't get you close to a beer, but can get you a tasty drink from their 1947 soda fountain. Patti has been running the place since her Daddy passed in November 2006, and is an excellent hostess and storyteller. Candy for just a few cents, ice cream concoctions in many flavors, old fashioned malts and sodas… enjoy!

CANOEING/CAMPING CHECKLIST

Bug Spray

Suntan Lotion/block

Plastic Drop Cloths (Rain)

Trash Bags

Dry (Waterproof) Bags

Ziplocks

Water /food

Forks/plates

Batteries.

Nose Strips (For Our Loud Friends) Ear Plugs (See Nose Strips)

Reynolds Wrap (Grub Leftover)

Small Pillow

Large Ziplocks

First Aid Kit

Sleeping Bag

Tent

Knife

Clothesline Rope

Pots/pans/large Spoon

Grill/grate

Fire Starter/matches

Blankets

2 Sets Of Keys

River Shoes/dry Shoes

Thermarest/air Mattress

River and Dry Clothes

Bungee Cords

Cooler, Ice, Water

Frisbees

Dry (Waterproof) Box

Rain Poncho

Flashlights

Towels

Soap, Toothpaste/brush

Toilet Paper

Euchre Decks

Can Opener

Camera and Film

Aspirin

River Chairs

Baseball Cap

$$$ and Wallet

Handtowel/paper Plates

Sunglasses
Vicks VapoRub (deer flies hate the smell)

AUTRAIN RIVER
AuTrain River Canoe and Kayak Rental 906-892-8367
N7163 Forest Lake Rd, AuTrain, MI 49806
http://autrainrivercanoes.com

Northwoods Resort 906-892-8114
N7070 Forest Lake Rd, AuTrain, MI 49806
http://www.northwoodsresort.net/

BETE GRISE RIVER
Keweenaw Adventure Company 906-289-4303
155 Gratiot Street, Copper Harbor, MI 49918
www.keweenawadventure.com

BRULE RIVER
Michi-Aho Resort 906-875-3514
2181 M-69, Crystal Falls, MI 49920
www.michi-aho.com

Northwoods Wilderness Outfitters 906-774-9009, 1-800-530-8859
N-4088 Pine Mountain Road, Iron Mountain, MI 49801
http://www.northwoodsoutfitters.com/

Paddlers and Pedalers 906-284-3438
32 W. Adams Street, Iron River, MI 49935
http://www.paddlersandpedalersllc.com/

ESCANABA RIVER
Soaring Eagle Outfitters 906-346-9142, 877-346-9142
93 N. Pine Street, Gwinn, MI 49841
http://www.uppelletstoves.com/upanimals.html

Uncle Ducky Outfitters 906-228-5447, 877-228-5447
434 E. Prospect, Marquette, MI 49855
http://www.uncleduckyoutfitters.com/

FOX RIVER
Big Cedar Campground & Canoe Livery 906-586-6684
7936 State Hwy. M-77, Germfask, MI 49836
http://www.bigcedarcampground.com/

Northland Outfitters 906-586-9801, 800-808-3FUN
8174 Hwy M-77, Germfask, MI 49836
http://www.northoutfitters.com/

LAKE SUPERIOR/PICTURED ROCKS/ISLE ROYALE
Keweenaw Adventure Company 906-289-4303
155 Gratiot Street, Copper Harbor, MI 49918
http://www.keweenawadventure.com/

Northern Waters Adventures 906-387-2323
712 West Munising Avenue, Munising, MI 49862
www.northernwaters.com

Paddling Michigan 906-228-5447
321 South Lakeshore Blvd, Marquette, MI 49855
www.paddlingmichigan.com

LES CHENEAUX ISLANDS
Woods and Water Ecotours 906-484-4157
20 S. Pickford Ave., Hessel, MI 49745
http://upecotours.com/

MANISTIQUE RIVER
Big Cedar Campground & Canoe Livery 906-586-6684
7936 State Hwy. M-77, Germfask, MI 49836
http://www.bigcedarcampground.com/

Northland Outfitters 906-586-9801, 800-808-3FUN
8174 Hwy M-77, Germfask, MI 49836
http://www.northoutfitters.com/

MENOMINEE RIVER
Northwoods Adventures 906-563-5450 (whitewater rafting trips)
N-4017 N Highway US 2, Iron Mountain, MI 49801
www.michiganrafts.com

Northwoods Wilderness Outfitters 906-774-9009, 1-800-530-8859
N-4088 Pine Mountain Road, Iron Mountain, MI 49801
http://www.northwoodsoutfitters.com/

MICHIGAMME RIVER
Michi-Aho Resort 906-875-3514
2181 M-69, Crystal Falls, MI 49920
www.michi-aho.com/

Northwoods Wilderness Outfitters 906-774-9009, 1 800 530 8859
N-4088 Pine Mountain Road, Iron Mountain, MI 49801
http://www.northwoodsoutfitters.com/

Uncle Ducky Outfitters 906-228-5447, 877-228-5447
434 E. Prospect, Marquette, MI 49855
http://www.uncleduckyoutfitters.com/

ONTONAGON RIVER
Sylvania Outfitters, Inc. 906-358-4766
E23423 Hwy. 2, Watersmeet, MI 49969
http://www.sylvaniaoutfitters.com/

PAINT RIVER
Michi-Aho Resort 906-875-3514
2181 M-69, Crystal Falls, MI 49920
www.michi-aho.com

Northwoods Wilderness Outfitters 906-774-9009, 1-800-530-8859
N-4088 Pine Mountain Road, Iron Mountain, MI 49801
http://www.northwoodsoutfitters.com/

Paddlers and Pedalers 906-284-3438
32 W. Adams Street, Iron River, MI 49935
http://www.paddlersandpedalersllc.com/

PORTAGE RIVER
Year Round Gear 906-828-9191
220 Shelden Avenue, Houghton, MI 49931
www.yearroundgear.com

STURGEON RIVER
Year Round Gear 906-828-9191
220 Shelden Avenue, Houghton, MI 49931
www.yearroundgear.com

169

TAHQUAMEMON RIVER
Tahquamenon General Store Canoe & Kayak Rentals 906-492-3560
39991 W. Highway 123, Paradise, MI 49768
genestahquamenongeneralstore.com

The Woods 906-203-7624
P.O. Box 536, Newberry, MI 49868
www.thewoodscanoerental.net

TWO HEARTED RIVER
North Store Outpost (across from Wolf Inn) 906-658-3450
18383 County Road 407 (Deer Park Road)
Newberry, MI 49868
http://www.michigan.org/property/north-store-outpost/

MICHIGAN CANOE & KAYAK LIVERIES – LOWER PENINSULA RIVERS
(check www.canoeingmichiganrivers.com for updates)

AUSABLE RIVER
Alcona Canoe Rental & Campground 989-735-2973, 800-526-7080
6351 Bamfield Road, Glennie, MI 48737
http://www.alconacanoes.com/

Bear Paw Cabins & Canoe Livery 989-826-3313
3744 W. M72, Luzerne, MI 48636
http://www.bearpawcabinsandcanoes.com/

Borcher's Ausable Canoe Livery
989-348-4921, 800-762-8756
101 Maple St., Grayling, MI 49738
http://www.canoeborchers.com/

Carlisle Canoe Livery 989-344-1400
110 State St, Grayling, MI 49738
http://www.carlislecanoelivery.com/

Gott's Landing 989-826-3411, 888-226-8748(Reservations only)
701 N. Morenci Rd., Mio, MI 48647
http://www.gottslanding.com/

Hinchman Acres 989-826-3267, 800-438-0203
702 N. M-33, P. O. Box 220, Mio, MI 48647
http://www.hinchman.com

Hunt's Canoes 989-739-4408
711 Lake Street, Oscoda, MI 48750
www.huntscanoes.com

Jim's Canoe (989) 348-3203
1706 Wakeley Bridge Rd., Grayling, MI 49738
http://www.jimscanoe.com/

Oscoda Canoe Rental 989-739-9040
678 River Rd., Oscoda, MI 48750
http://www.oscodacanoe.com/

Penrod's AuSable River Resort 888-467-4837, 989-348-2910
100 Maple St., Grayling, MI 49738
http://www.penrodscanoe.com/

Rainbow Resort 989-826-3423
731 Camp Ten Road, Mio, MI 48647
http://www.rainbowresortmio.com/

Rollway Resort 989-728-3322
6160 Rollways Road, Hale, MI 48739
http://www.rollwayresort.com/

AUSABLE, SOUTH BRANCH
Campbell's Canoeing 989-275-5810, 800-722-6633
1112 Lake St., Roscommon, MI 48653
http://www.canoeatcampbells.com/

Paddle Brave Canoe Livery & Campground 989-275-5273, 800-681-7092
10610 Steckert Bridge Rd., Roscommon, MI 48653
http://www.paddlebrave.com/

Parmalee Trading Post 989-826-3543
78 N. Red Oak Rd, Lewiston, MI 49756
http://www.parmaleetradingpost.net/

BEAR RIVER
Bear River Canoe Livery 231-347-9038, 231-838-4141
2517 McDougal, Petosky, MI 49770
http://www.bearrivercanoelivery.com/

BETSIE RIVER
Alvina's Canoe and Boat Rental 231-276-9514
6470 Betsie River Rd. S, Interlochen, MI 49643
http://www.michigan.org/property/alvina-s-canoe-boat-livery/

Betsie River Canoes & Campground 231- 879-3850
13598 Lindy Rd./Highway 602, Thompsonville, MI 49683
http://www.michigan.org/property/betsie-river-canoes-campground

Crystal Adventures Lodging & Rentals 231-651-9648
17227 Vondra Road, Thompsonville, MI 49683
www.crystaladventures.com

Hanmer's Riverside Resort 231-882-7783
2251 Benzie Hwy, Benzonia, MI 49616
http://hanmers.com/

Trading Post 231-325-2202
8294 Deadstream Road, Honor, MI 49640
www.canoeplatteriver.com

Turtle Lake Campground 231-275-7353
854 Miller Road, Beulah, MI 49617
http://turtlelakecampground.com/

Vacation Trailer Park Inc. 231-882-5101
2080 Benzie Hwy., Benzonia, MI 49616
http://www.vacationtrailer.com/

BLACK RIVER (Bangor-South Haven)
Kayak Kayak 616-366-1146
321 Douglas Ave., Holland, MI 49424
www.kayak-kayak.com

BLACK RIVER (Croswell)
Black River Kayak Rental 810-304-2951
43 N Howard Ave., Croswell, MI 48422
www.blackriverkayaks.com

BLACK RIVER (Northern Lower Peninsula)
Black River Canoe Outfitters/Ma & Pa's Country Store
989-733-8054   M33 & Hackett Lake Rd., Onaway, MI 49765

BOARDMAN RIVER
Ranch Rudolf 231-947-9529
6841 Brown Bridge Rd., Traverse City, MI 49686
http://www.ranchrudolf.com/
The River 231-334-7888
5959 South Oak Street, Glen Arbor, MI 49636
http://therivertc.com/

BOYNE RIVER
Boyne River Adventures 231-459-6990
230 Water Street, Boyne City, MI 49712
www.boyneriveradventures.com

CEDAR RIVER
Cedar River Canoe Trips 989-387-8658
12 East M61, Gladwin, MI 48624
www.gladwinboatrental.com

Ike's Mobile Kayak Rentals 989-750-5251
Midland, MI 48640
www.ikeskayaks.com

CHIPPEWA RIVER
Buckley's Mountainside Canoes 989-772-5437
4700 W. Remus Rd., Mt. Pleasant, MI 48858
http://www.buckleyscanoe.com/

Chippewa River Outfitters 989-772-5474, 888-775-6077
3763 S. Lincoln Rd., Mt Pleasant, MI 48858
http://www.chipoutfitters.com/

Ike's Mobile Kayak Rentals 989-750-5251
Midland, MI 48640
www.ikeskayaks.com

CLAM RIVER
new livery coming soon on... Main Street, Lake City, MI 49651

CLINTON RIVER
Clinton River Canoe & Kayak Rentals; Outdoor Escorts LLC 248-421-3445
916 Highlander, Lake Orion, MI 48362
www.outdoorescorts.com

COLDWATER RIVER
GR Paddling 616-558-2609
217 Leyden Avenue SW, Grand Rapids, MI 49504
www.grpaddling.com

Indian Valley 616-891-8579
8200 108th, Middleville, MI 49333
http://www.indianvalleycampgroundandcanoe.com/

CROCKERY CREEK
GR Paddling 616-558-2609
217 Leyden Avenue SW, Grand Rapids, MI 49504
www.grpaddling.com

Lakeshore Kayak Rental 616-566-1325
15348 Cleveland Street, Spring Lake, MI 49456
www.lakeshorekayakrental.com

CROOKED RIVER
BrassWind Landing 231-238-4843
6240 Mack Avenue, Indian River, MI 49749
www.artsandadventure.com

CRYSTAL RIVER
Crystal River Outfitters 231-334-4420
6249 W. River Rd., Glen Arbor, MI 49696
http://www.crystalriveroutfitters.com/

The River 231-334-7888
5959 South Oak Street, Glen Arbor, MI 49636
http://therivertc.com/

DOWAGIAC RIVER
Doe-Wah-Jack's Canoe Rental Inc. 888-782-7410, 269-782-7410
52963 M-51 N., Dowagiac, MI 49047
http://www.paddledcri.com/

FAWN RIVER
Fawn River Kayak Guide & Rental 269-625-0733
30749 Fawn Lake Road, Sturgis, MI 49091

Liquid Therapy Canoe & Kayak Rentals 269-273-9000
221 S. Main St., Three Rivers, MI 49093
https://sites.google.com/site/liquidtherapycanoeandkayak/

FLAT RIVER
Black Hawk Canoe Rental 616-581-4265
660 Whites Bridge Road, Belding, MI 48809
www.blackhawkcanoerental.com

Double R Ranch Resort 616-794-0520
4424 Whites Bridge Rd., Belding, MI 48809
http://www.doublerranch.com/

GR Paddling 616-558-2609
217 Leyden Avenue SW, Grand Rapids, MI 49504
www.grpaddling.com

FLINT RIVER
Good Ol' Redbeard's General Store 810-210-7602
114 E. Main Street, Flushing, MI 48433
http://redbeardsauction.com/canoes

GALIEN RIVER
Galien River Kayaking 888-932-4575
17440 Red Arrow Hwy, New Buffalo, MI 49117
http://galienriverkayaking.com/
Outpost Sports 269-637-5555
114 Dyckman, South Haven, MI 49090
www.outpostsports.com

GRAND RIVER
Burchfield Park 616-676-2233
881 Grovenburg Road, Holt, MI 48842
http://pk.ingham.org/Parks/BurchfieldPark.aspx

GR Paddling 616-558-2609
217 Leyden Avenue SW, Grand Rapids, MI 49504
www.grpaddling.com

Grand Fish 517-410-0801
530 River Street, Lansing, MI 48933
www.thegrandfish.com

Grand Kayak 517-490-0820
13920 State Road, Grand Ledge, MI 48837
www.grandkayak.com

Grand River Canoe and Kayak 616-528-4077
327 Hogadorn Pl SW, Grand Rapids, MI 49504
http://grandriverkayakandcanoe.com

Lakeshore Kayak Rental 616-566-1325
15348 Cleveland Street, Spring Lake, MI 49456
www.lakeshorekayakrental.com

Quiet Water Sports 517-879-8981
551 Avenue A
Vandercook Lake (Jackson), MI 49203
www.quietworldsports.com

River Town Adventures 517-253-7523
325 City Market Drive, Lansing, MI 48912
www.rivertownadventures.com

HERSEY RIVER
Hersey Canoe Livery 231-832-7220
625 E. 4th St., Hersey, MI 49639

HURON RIVER
Argo Canoe Livery 734-794-6241
1055 Longshore Drive, Ann Arbor, MI 48105
www.a2gov.org/canoe

Gallup Canoe Livery 734-794-6240
3000 Fuller Road, Ann Arbor, MI 48105
www.a2gov.org/canoe

H2E River Adventures 734-379-9912
36495 W. Jefferson Ave., Rockwood, MI 48173
http://www.h2eriveradventures.com/

Heavner Canoe Rental 248-685-2379
2775 Garden Rd., Milford, MI 48381
http://www.heavnercanoe.com/

Motor City Canoe Rental 313-473-9847
37205 Pointe Mouille Rd.
Brownstown Charter Twp, MI 48173
https://www.motorcitycanoerental.com/

Skip's Huron River Canoe Livery 734-768-8686
3780 Delhi Ct., Ann Arbor, MI 48103
http://skipshuronrivercanoeliveryllc.com/

Village Canoe Rental 248-685-9207
1216 Garden, Milford, MI 48381
http://villagecanoe.com/

INDIAN RIVER
BrassWind Landing 231-238-4843
6240 Mack Avenue, Indian River, MI 49749
www.artsandadventure.com

JORDAN RIVER
Jordan Valley Outfitters 231-536-0006
311 N. Lake St. (M-66), East Jordan, MI 49727
http://www.jvoutfitters.com/

Swiss Hideaway, Inc 231-536-2341
1953 Graves Crossing, Mancelona, MI 49659
http://www.jordanriverfun.com/

KALAMAZOO RIVER
Kayak Kayak 616-366-1146
321 Douglas Ave., Holland, MI 49424
www.kayak-kayak.com

Lee's Adventure Sports 269-381-7700
311 W. Kilgore Road, Portage, MI 49002
http://www.leesadventuresports.com/

Marshall Recreation Department 269-781-5166
900 S. Marshall, Marshall, MI 49068
http://www.marshallrec.com/

Running Rivers Inc. 616-218-5021
Wade's Bayou Park, Douglas, MI 49406
http://www.running-rivers.info/

Twin Pines Campground and Canoe Livery 517-524-6298
9800 Wheeler Rd., Hanover, MI 49241
http://www.twinpinescampgrounds.org/

KAWKAWLIN RIVER
Ike's Mobile Kayak Rentals 989-750-5251
Midland, MI 48640
www.ikeskayaks.com

LAKE LEELANAU & LAKE MICHIGAN
Harbor House Trading Co. & Kayak Rentals 231-256-7530
101 N. Main Street, Leland, MI 49654
http://www.lelandharborhouse.com/

LITTLE MANISTEE RIVER
Enchanted Acres Campground 231-266-5102
9581 N. Brooks Rd., Irons, MI 49644
http://www.enchantedacrescamp.com/

Manistee Paddlesport Adventures 231-233-3265
231 Parkdale Avenue, Manistee, MI 49660
www.manisteepaddlesports.com
LITTLE MUSKEGON RIVER
Bob & Pat's White Birch Canoe Trips & Campground 231-328-4547
Paradise Rd., Falmouth, MI 49632
http://www.whitebirchcanoe.com/

Manistee Paddlesport Adventure 231-233-3265
231 Parkdale Avenue, Manistee, MI 49660
http://instalaunch.com/paddlesports/3235511

Wisner Rents Canoes 231-652-6743
25 W. Water St., Newaygo, MI 49337
http://www.wisnercanoes.com/

LOOKING GLASS RIVER
Grand Kayak 517-490-0820
13920 State Road, Grand Ledge, MI 48837
www.grandkayak.com

MANISTEE RIVER
Chippewa Landing 231-313-0832
10420 Chippewa Landing Trail, Manton, MI 49663
http://www.chippewalanding.com/

Enchanted Acres Campground 231-266-5102
9581 N. Brooks Rd., Irons, MI 49644
http://www.enchantedacrescamp.com/

Long's Canoe Livery 989-348-7224
2779 N. Manistee River Road, Grayling, MI 49738

Manistee Paddlesport Adventures 231-233-3265
231 Parkdale Avenue, Manistee, MI 49660
www.manisteepaddlesports.com

Pine River Paddlesports Center 231-862-3471
9590 Grand View Hwy. S37, Wellston, MI 49689
http://www.thepineriver.com/

Shel-Haven Canoe Rental 989-348-2158
P.O.Box 268, Grayling,MI 49738
http://shel-haven.com/

Smithville Landing 231-839-4579
M-66 on the Manistee River P.O.Box 341, Lake City, MI 49651
http://www.smithvillelanding.com/

Wilderness Canoe Trips 800-873-6379, 231-885-1485
6052 Riverview Rd., Mesick, MI 49668
http://www.manisteerivertrips.com/

MAPLE RIVER
Maple River Campground 989-981-6792
15420 French Rd., Pewamo, MI 48873
http://www.maplerivercampground.com/

MUSKEGON RIVER
Chinook Campground 231-834-7505
5741 W. 112th, Grant, MI 49327
www.chinookcampground.com

Croton Dam Float Trips 231-952-6037
5355 Croton Road, Newaygo, MI 49337

Duggan's Canoe Livery 989-539-7149
3100 N. Temple Drive, Harrison, MI 48625
http://www.dugganscanoes.com/

Guys Ultimate Kayak Service 231-740-0227
1241 Anna Road, Muskegon, MI 49445
http://www.guysultimatekayakservice.com/

Hersey Canoe Livery 231-832-7220
1596 Riverview Drive, Hersey, MI 49639
http://www.michigan.org/property/hersey-canoe-livery/

J & J's River Run 231-287-0008
205 E. 7th Street, Evart, MI 49631
http://www.jjriverrun.com/

Lakeshore Kayak Rental 616-566-1325
15348 Cleveland Street, Spring Lake, MI 49456
www.lakeshorekayakrental.com

Mystery Creek Campground 231-652-6915
9570 S. Wisner, Newaygo, MI 49337
www.chinookcamping.com

Putters Creek 231-744-1418
40 N. Causeway, North Muskegon, MI 49445
http://www.putterscreek.com/kayaks.html

Old Log Resort 231-743-2775
12062 M-115, Marion, MI 49665
https://oldlogresort.com/

River Country Campground 231-734-3808
6281 River Rd., Evart, MI 49631
http://www.campandcanoe.com/

River Rat Canoe Rental 231-834-9411
8702 River Dr. Bridgeton Twnshp, Grant, MI 49327
http://www.riverratcanoerental.com/

Salmon Run Campground & Vic's Canoes 231-834-5495
8845 Felch Ave., Grant, MI 49327
http://www.salmonrunmi.com/

Sawmill Tube and Canoe Livery 231-796-6408
230 Baldwin St., Big Rapids, MI 49307
http://www.sawmillbr.com/

White Birch Canoe Trips & Campground 231-328-4547
Paradise Rd., Falmouth, MI 49632
http://www.whitebirchcanoe.com/

Wisner Rents Canoes 231-652-6743
25 W. Water St., Newaygo, MI 49337
http://www.wisnercanoes.com/

OCQUEOC RIVER
Ocqueoc Outfitters 989-245-7204 or 989-734-4208
15524 US23 N at the Ocqueoc River, Ocqueoc, MI 49759
http://ocqueocoutfitters1.weebly.com/

PAW PAW RIVER
Paw Paw River Campgrounds & Canoes 269-463-5454
5355 Michigan Hwy 140, Watervliet, MI 49098
www.pawpawrivercampgroundandcanoes.com

Paw Paw River Kayaking 888-932-4575
601 Graham Ave, Benton Harbor, MI 49022
www.pawpawriverkayaking.com

PENTWATER RIVER
Pentwater River Outfitters 231-869-2999
22 S. Hancock Street, Pentwater, MI 49449
www.pentwaterriveroutfitters.com

PERE MARQUETTE RIVER
Baldwin Canoe Rental 231-745-4669, 800-272-3642
9117 South M37, P. O. Box 269, Baldwin, MI 49304
http://www.baldwincanoe.com/

Henry's Landing & Canoe Livery 231-757-0101
701 S. Main Street, Scottville, MI 49454
www.henryslanding.com

Pere Marquette Expeditions/Nelson's Frontier Market, 231-845-7285
1649 South Pere Marquette Hwy, Ludington, MI 49431 www.pmexpeditions.com
River Run Canoe Livery 231-757-2266
600 S Main St., Scottville, MI 49454
http://www.riverruncanoerental.com/

PIGEON RIVER (Northern-Lower Pennisula)
Big Bear Adventures 231-238-8181
4271 S. Straits Hwy., Indian River, MI 49749
http://www.bigbearadventures.com/

BrassWind Landing 231-238-4843
6240 Mack Avenue, Indian River, MI 49749
www.artsandadventure.com

PIGEON RIVER (by Grand Haven))
Kayak Kayak 616-366-1146
321 Douglas Ave., Holland, MI 49424
www.kayak-kayak.com

Lakeshore Kayak Rental 616-566-1325
15348 Cleveland Street, Spring Lake, MI 49456
www.lakeshorekayakrental.com

174

PIGEON RIVER (by Three Rivers)
Liquid Therapy Canoe & Kayak Rentals 269-273-9000
221 S. Main St., Three Rivers, MI 49093
https://sites.google.com/site/liquidtherapycanoeandkayak/

PINEBOG RIVER
Tip-O-Thumb Canoe & Kayak Rental 989-738-7656
2471 Port Austin Rd., Port Austin, MI 48467
http://www.michigan.org/property/tip-o-thumb-canoe-kayak-rental/

PINE RIVER
Bosman Canoe Rental 877-6canoes
M55 & M37, Wellston, MI 49689
www.bosmancanoe.com

Enchanted Acres Campground 231-266-5102
9581 N. Brooks Rd., Irons, MI 49644
http://www.enchantedacrescamp.com/

Horina Canoe & Kayak Rental 231-862-3470
9889 M-37 South, Wellston, Michigan 49689
http://www.michigan.org/property/horina-canoe-kayak-rental/

Pine River Paddlesports Center 231-862-3471
9590 Grand View Hwy. S37, Wellston, MI 49689
http://www.thepineriver.com/

Shomler Canoes & Kayaks 231-862-3475
11390 N. M-37, Irons, MI 49644
http://www.shomlercanoes.com/

Sportsman's Port Canoes, Campground 231- 862-3571, 888-226-6301
10487 W. M55 Hwy., Wellston, MI 49689
http://www.sportsmansport.com/

River Rat Canoe and Camping, 231-862-3475
7892 S. M37, Wellston, MI 49689

PINE RIVER (mid-Michigan Pine, near Midland)
Ike's Mobile Kayak Rentals 989-750-5251
Midland, MI 48640
www.ikeskayaks.com

PLATTE RIVER
Honor Canoe Rental 231-325-0112
2212 Valley Road/US-31, Honor, MI 49640
www.honorcanoerentals.com/

Riverside Canoes 231-325-5622
5042 Scenic Hwy., Honor, MI 49640
http://www.canoemichigan.com/

Trading Post 231-325-2202
8294 Deadstream Road, Honor, MI 49640
www.canoeplatteriver.com

PORTAGE RIVER & PRAIRIE RIVER
Liquid Therapy Canoe & Kayak Rentals 269-273-9000
221 S. Main St., Three Rivers, MI 49093
https://sites.google.com/site/liquidtherapycanoeandkayak/

RED CEDAR RIVER
River Town Adventures 517-253-7523
325 City Market Drive, Lansing, MI 48912
www.rivertownadventures.com

RIFLE RIVER
Big Mike's Canoe Rental 989-473-3444
2595 Shady Shores Rd., Lupton, MI 48635
http://www.michigan.org/property/big-mike-s-canoe-rental

Outdoor Adventures 989-654-3195
334 Melita Rd., Sterling, MI 48659
http://www.outdooradventuresinc.com/rifle-river-resort-sterling-mi/

Rifle River Campground & Canoe Livery 989-654-2521
5825 Townline Road, Sterling, MI 48659
www.riflerivercampground.com

Russell Canoes & Campgrounds 989-653-2644
146 Carrington St., Omer, MI 48749
http://www.russellcanoe.com/

Troll Landing Campground & Canoe Livery 989-345-7260
2660 Rifle River Trail, West Branch, MI 48661
http://www.trolllanding.com/

White's Canoe Livery 989-654-2654
400 S. Melita, Sterling, MI 48659
http://www.michigan.org/property/white-s-canoe-livery

Whispering Pines Campground & Canoe Livery 989-653-3321
538 S. Hale (M65), Twining, MI 48766-9715
http://www.michigan.org/property/whispering-pines-campground-and-canoe-livery/

RIVER RAISIN
River Raisin Canoe Livery 734-529-9029
1151 Plank Rd., Dundee, MI 48131
http://www.riverraisincanoelivery.com/

Tecumseh Paddling Company 517-423-2700
703E. Chicago Blvd. (M50), Tecumseh, MI
www.tecumsehpaddle.com

ROCKY RIVER
Liquid Therapy Canoe & Kayak Rentals Inc. 269-273-9000
221 S. Main St., Three River, MI 49093
https://sites.google.com/site/liquidtherapycanoeandkayak/

ROGUE RIVER
AAA Canoe Rental 616-866-9264
525 Northland Dr., Rockford, MI 49341
http://www.aaacanoerental.com/

GR Paddling 616-558-2609
217 Leyden Avenue SW, Grand Rapids, MI 49504
www.grpaddling.com

Grand Rogue Campground and Canoe 616-361-1053
6400 West River Dr., Belmont, MI 49306
www.grandrogue.com

ROUGE RIVER
Heavner Canoe Rental 248-685-2379
2775 Garden Rd., Milford, MI 48381
http://www.heavnercanoe.com/

SHIAWASSEE RIVER
Cheff's Canoe Rental 989-494-9955 & 989-288-7067
Walnut Hills Campground, 7865 Lehring Rd, Durand, MI 48429
www.cheffscanoerental.com

SLEEPING BEAR DUNES - SHORELINE GUIDED TOURS
All About Water 269-214-4848
8995 South Kasson Street, Cedar, MI 49621
www.allaboutwaterusa.com

ST. JOSEPH RIVER
En Gedi Campground River Resort and Canoe Rental 269-689-7490
30321 Covey Road, Leonidas, MI 49066
http://www.engediresort.com/

Liquid Therapy Canoe & Kayak Rentals 269-273-9000
221 S. Main St., Three Rivers, MI 49093
https://sites.google.com/site/liquidtherapycanoeandkayak/

STURGEON RIVER
Big Bear Adventures 231-238-8181
4271 S. Straits Hwy., Indian River, MI 49749
http://www.bigbearadventures.com/

BrassWind Landing 231-238-4843
6240 Mack Avenue, Indian River, MI 49749
www.artsandadventure.com

Sturgeon River Paddlesports 231-525-6878
12961 S. Straits Hwy, Wolverine, MI 49799
www.sturgeonriverpaddle.com

THORNAPPLE RIVER
GR Paddling 616-558-2609
217 Leyden Avenue SW, Grand Rapids, MI 49504
www.grpaddling.com

Indian Valley 616-891-8579
8200 108th, Middleville, MI 49333
http://www.indianvalleycampgroundandcanoe.com/

U-Rent-Em Canoe Livery (269) 945-3191
805 W Apple St., Hastings, Michigan 49058
www.urentemcanoe.com

Whispering Waters Campground and Canoes 269-945-5166
1805 N. Irving Rd., Hastings, MI 49058
http://www.whisperingwatersonline.com/

THUNDER BAY RIVER
Adventureland Sports 989-255-7796
P.O. Box 694 (at Duck Park, cor. Long Rapids at Chisholm), Alpena, MI 49707
www.adventurelandsports.com

Campers Cove Campground and Canoe 888-306-3708, 989-356-3708
5005 Long Rapids Rd., Alpena, MI 49707
http://www.camperscovecampground.com/

TITTABAWASSEE RIVER
Cedar River Canoe Trips 989-387-8658
12 East M61, Gladwin, MI 48624
www.gladwinboatrental.com

Ike's Mobile Kayak Rentals 989-750-5251
Midland, MI 48640
www.ikeskayaks.com

WHITE RIVER
Happy Mohawk Canoe Livery 231-894-4209
735 Fruitvale Rd., Montague, MI 49437
http://www.happymohawk.com/

Doc Fletcher was born Jeffrey Marc Fletcher in Detroit, Michigan, in 1954. He moved with his family to Lambertville, Michigan, in 1967, graduating in 1972 from Bedford High School – Go Mules! Doc is a proud Eastern Michigan University Huron, where he fell in love with his future bride before graduating from the University in 1976 with a Bachelor's degree in Marketing. Doc took his first canoe trip in 1978 on the Pere Marquette River, and ever since then gets back into a canoe whenever possible. He enjoyed a rewarding 30 year career as an account executive with the folks at Duracell, the battery company, from 1976 to 2006.

Weekend Canoeing In Michigan was his first book.
Doc lives in Northville with his wife Maggie Meeker - the coed he first saw on his 20th birthday while both attended EMU.